A Perfect WALK

One Man's Lifelong Struggle with Anxiety, OCD, and Suicidal Thoughts

PAUL M. GALLAGHER

A Perfect Walk

ISBN 978-1-7352823-0-5

Editing and design services by ChristianEditingServices.com.

Author photo by Rex Keep Photography.

Table of Contents

Preface

This book is not fiction. I am welcoming you into the mind of a (previously) mentally ill individual. I want to have an open and honest conversation on mental health. Debilitating anxiety and distress are reality for millions of people. Just in the U.S. alone,

> In any given year approximately 40 million Americans will suffer from a debilitating encounter with anxiety. Over the course of your lifetime, there's a 25% chance you'll experience a diagnosable anxiety disorder.[1]

Writing about the reality of my life struggles with anxiety was difficult, but the journey was therapeutic. Thank you for coming along for the read.

Millions of people with mental health issues suffer in silence for various reasons, including pride and the fear of being stigmatized. For many years I was afraid to open up about my struggles because I thought others might consider me crazy or weird. I was terrified of such demoralizing labels. But my attitude, actions, words, and poor decision making gave good reasons for others to think poorly of me.

My good friend Jason Eddie Nowak and I first discussed this book becoming reality in 2004 when we met in

---

1 Mel Schwartz, L.C.S.W., "Getting Unstuck: Overcoming Anxiety and Distress." Last updated December 21, 2018. *Psychology Today: https://www.psychologytoday.com/us/blog/shift-mind/201812/getting-unstuck-overcoming-anxiety-and-distress* (January 6, 2020).

Greendale, Wisconsin. I had just completed treatment for obsessive-compulsive disorder (OCD) at Rogers Memorial Hospital in Oconomowoc, Wisconsin. For ten-plus years I talked of writing this book. Many years later, here we are with the book in hand. Yes, procrastination is one of several issues I excel at.

As you'll see, I often struggle with what I call the Negative Ps: pride, perfection, and procrastination. Pride is my biggest downfall. Perfection is unattainable. Procrastination leads to frustration. I know these well and I've come to know we're to be humble rather than prideful or boastful. My perfectionist tendency is what drove my procrastination. It wasn't easy to write this book; I wrote little by little and it took me eight years (2012–2019). And that's okay. I've learned not to expect change to occur overnight. A lot of life comes down to what I refer to as the Positive Ps: planning, preparation, persistence, perseverance, and patience. I finished writing *A Perfect Walk* at age forty-five so it covers a lot of territory about my life and experiences.

I was raised in a neighborhood in Greendale, a suburb of Milwaukee, and naturally became a Green Bay Packers fan. I also became a sports junkie—make that a fanatic. As I did when coaching baseball, I've woven in some life lessons. I lived in lies for so long; now it's time for me to share the truth with love. I hope you'll enjoy reading my true story as much as I've enjoyed writing it.

Acknowledgements

Thank you to the many people who assisted me in writing and publishing this long-awaited book.

To my best friend and sister, Michelle. You are well aware of my battle with guilt, shame, anger, anxiety, depression, and the lies I told myself from a very young age. You know the severe social anxiety that plagued me as early as age four each time I left home for swim lessons. Thank you for standing by me.

To my good friend Heath Talbot. You were always there, holding me accountable. Thank you.

Thank you, readers, for choosing this book. If you're struggling with mental health issues, I hope my experiences will help you—or at least guide you in the right direction for quality help. Maybe you can then help others in similar need, creating a positive domino effect among the people in your sphere of influence who are struggling with mental and emotional wellbeing. This life is tough, but we are not alone.

INTRODUCTION

A Perfect Walk is an honest personal testimony of my struggles with mental and emotional health. I wrote this book to help others in similar battles and to help cleanse my mind of the anxiety, anger, guilt, and shame that resulted from a traumatic and serious eye injury I suffered at age four. This book is not about saving one's vision, though that is important. It's about saving one's soul. I am simply inviting you into the mind of an emotionally and mentally ill individual.

Because of the injury and a dysfunctional childhood, I became extraordinarily anxious and unable to forgive others. I allowed my emotional anguish as a child to continue well into adulthood. I held grudges and wasn't able to communicate openly. My poor choices, including excessive drinking, addiction, and immorality, adversely affected my day-to-day life, health, and relationships. I was unable to forgive myself and to accept fallibility as a normal human characteristic.

When we learn that what we're doing is wrong, the conviction we experience is intended for positive reasons: to strengthen our knowledge, morality, health, healing, and overall wellbeing. I experienced much guilt—and forgiveness—over my poor choices, and I came to understand that many of my mental and emotional concerns could be pinned on only one person: me. I was my problem.

For many years I tried to be perfect in tasks, even when

doing simple things like walking my dog, Bruno (1999–2011). I would essentially try to take what I considered to be a perfect walk (thus the book title), leaving at an exact time, on the dot. Whenever I was a minute late getting started, I had a panic attack in the form of chest pain, stomach discomfort, and racing thoughts. At times I'd call off the walk altogether, believing I was too late to pursue it because I had already "failed." That was just one of many lies I told myself from a young age. I often subscribed to the mentality of perfectionism, regardless of my goals. Not only would I need to start the walk precisely at 8:00 p.m., for example, but I'd also need to wear the same jogging suit and shoes each time. My shoestrings had to be an exact length, double-knotted, and otherwise tied a specific way. Once outside, I wanted my strides to be perfect. I wanted to breathe, walk, and think perfectly. At that time, I didn't know the term "obsessive-compulsive."

Stepping on a crack in the sidewalk also caused me anxiety. Bruno and I couldn't go off the perfect path without my stomach pain kicking in—a physical symptom of the severe anxiety I battled for many years. I was also extremely paranoid on walks. I was afraid that people driving by would yell out profanities, obscenities, or other rude things. I lived in victim mentality.

I've concealed my mental battles for most of my life, but I've found that hiding truth doesn't do anyone any good. The truth is, none of us is perfect; as humans, we'll never achieve perfection—and that's perfectly normal. As I'll demonstrate in *A Perfect Walk*, what's positive and healthy is to be persistent in simply developing and maintaining good and balanced habits. The truth—learning, acknowledging, and embracing truth—does indeed make us free.

1

The Gift of Life

I was born in Milwaukee on December 31, 1973, and named after my Uncle Paul. His life was cut very short—he died of leukemia at age three. The wisdom he had at such a young age would take me four decades to grasp. On his deathbed, Uncle Paul said to his mother, "Don't worry, Mommy, just look at all the pretties." Powerful words. What he must have been seeing at the edge of his earthly life has increased my hope in eternal life.

It's amazing to think how we each got here in the first place—conception, cell multiplication, birth. Why do we worry so much? Worry is a waste of precious time. As I've grown into middle age, I've seen more certainly how short this present life is.

> **Life Lesson #1:** Life is a gift, too short to waste time in worry. You can either enjoy or destroy your life by how you choose to view and use your

> experiences. Practice making the most of every moment. I encourage you to become familiar with the term *mindfulness*.

That shared, I confess I still battle the tendency to mercilessly beat myself up for past mistakes. We must forget the past and look forward to what lies ahead!

At age four I suffered a blunt-force injury to my right eye. A neighbor boy and I were having a stick-throwing contest in his backyard. I'd been warned about playing with sticks but being just four—and having a fascination with sticks—I didn't listen.

We were seeing who could throw a stick farther. I was right behind him when he drew his stick back to throw it. The next thing I knew, one of his older siblings was carrying me to my house. Then someone was driving me to the hospital. I can still remember sitting in the backseat. In the emergency room, an ophthalmologist determined I had suffered a serious injury to my right eye.

> **Life Lesson #2:** Do *not* play with sticks!

That event led me into fear, anxiety, regret, frustration, anger, and resentment—and eventually into greater anxiety and deeper depression. In the aftermath of the accident, a number of incidents surrounding it fostered in me an inability for many years to forgive the neighbor boy and his parents. My determined stance of unforgiveness made it easier for me to hold grudges against others through the years. I was also angry at God for allowing the accident to happen. I chose anger and resentment for a long time—thirty-plus years of unforgiveness. It wasn't until age thirty-eight that I decided to deal with my unaddressed emotions. By that time, my spirit was very ill.

> **Life Lesson #3:** Don't hold grudges. Forgiveness is healing and freeing.

In 2012, trying to make a positive in life from a negative, I wrote the following article to a patient advocate for healthy vision. I relayed the details of the accident and concluded with these words:

> I have gone through life bitter, angry, and frustrated over what transpired that day in 1978 and over having to wear eyeglasses. The right lens is very thick due to the weak vision in that injured eye. Without the lens correction, I believe my right eye vision is 20/800. Classmates would often ask to try on my eyeglasses, curious about the thickness of the right lens. Though I'd let them try my eyeglasses, deep down I was really upset that they viewed my circumstance as a novelty. Maybe by saying yes to them I was looking for a pity party.
>
> I was also angry and frustrated when playing sports and doing other things because I really wished I didn't have to wear eyeglasses. What's the bottom line? Please stress the importance of not playing with sticks and the importance of people—all ages—wearing protective eyewear when playing sports. One can suffer vision loss playing football, basketball, racquetball, baseball . . . In fact, during a Green Bay Packers' game, their quarterback took a defender's hand to the face. The rival's hand inadvertently wedged into the quarterback's mask and caught his right eye. The injured player had to sit out of the game for a few minutes. Thank God his eye was okay. Just like that, in the snap of a finger, a person's vision can be lost.
>
> Having lost considerable vision myself, it pains me

to see anyone suffer an eye injury. Out of my pain a passion was birthed for educating others on the importance of eye care and protection.

I hope this article is beneficial to you. Thank you for your time, and God bless you all as you continue to educate others on this important topic.

— Paul M. Gallagher

2

Hindsight is 20/20

Life Lesson #4: Don't take your health for granted.

For reasons we won't always understand, we each suffer physical and emotional injuries in life. It's often in hindsight that we see how our suffering can be used for good.

I believe God continues to use my eye injury for several reasons. First, my experience can help prevent others from suffering a similar injury. I'm the poster child for protective eye care. Second, my years of mental and emotional anxiety brought me eye to eye with God's profound, life-changing truths. Third, I have a desire to share those truths with others. As a baseball coach, I saw junior high and high school kids on the same path of lies, anger, and anxiety that I suffered. I'm purposed to deposit truth and hope into their minds with the desire they will learn earlier on how to thrive rather than simply survive. My experiences are meant to offer emotional and spiritual courage to anyone who feels hopeless so they might choose to avoid the major pitfalls I dwelled in for too many years.

The first truth I had to acknowledge was that I had anger issues. The intensive anger I clung to resulted in severe anxiety. I've long been fidgety and afraid and I tend to be on high alert at all times: hypervigilant. I jump easily at the smallest things.

I then had to recognize that I needed to address those anger issues honestly if I truly wanted my diminishing mental, emotional, and spiritual health to change for the better. I wanted that desperately.

Finally, I had to practice forgiving others and myself. I had learned from age four to carry a deep grudge against my childhood friend and his parents. A lawsuit against their home insurance company in 1994 created even more animosity between our two families, which lasted for many years. I grew up in that animosity. As I grew older and wiser, I realized the freeing and healing importance of forgiveness. But when I took those first steps, I felt I was forgiving them because I was *supposed* to rather than out of a heart of true forgiveness.

> **Life Lesson #5:** Forgiveness is mandatory for your own emotional and mental healing. Forgiveness is a choice and a process of practice that often requires steel dedication and time to move from head to heart.

At the time of my injury, I was laid up in bed for a while. My eye doctor stopped by to check on me a couple of times. He was a good guy and a blessing. In May 2015, after sending him a release request for my medical records, I received the following response.

Dear Paul:

I wish you well with your book in attempts to find out some of your root causes of anxiety. I think it will be a very helpful journey for you.

I have reviewed all your records, and in addition to what I send you, I am enclosing a letter that was sent by another doctor, which was prepared for a lawyer back in 1994. This gives quite a detailed chronology and his impressions on the injury. My notes will be a little different and will give us more of an overview.

We met on November 9, 1978 after you were brought to my office after you were hit in the right eye with a stick while playing with the neighbor boy. No one had witnessed the incident. You had an abrasion along with bleeding in front of your iris, inside the eye and blood inside the back behind the natural lens of the eye, what we call vitreous. There was also some bruising of your lids. The abrasion healed and there was a slow resolution of the vitreous hemorrhage. You were kept at home and I visited you a couple of times during the early period.

Soon after, I could see that there was a scar by the upper part of your nerve in the back and the blood had largely cleared. I could start to see then that the blow to your eye had disrupted the supporting fibers—called zonules—of your natural lens up in the corner by your nose to where the vitreous, "jelly of the eye," was coming through that space around the lens into the front of the natural lens. As I continued to follow you, your vision by December 21st had improved to 20/30 and by March 1979, 20/40 with glass correction. The injury made that eye near-sighted because of the displacement of the natural lens, whereas your left eye had good vision without any correction. You were not very compliant about wearing the eyeglasses. This would be a normal response for a young child since your left eye could see perfectly fine. The pupil on that right eye was larger than the left eye from the injury. I could see the zonular ruptures in the upper inner corner and that the lens had been pushed back from its normal position and had shifted down and out. I was aware of the damage in 1978, but it was very evident by 1980. Your correction for near-sightedness had increased gradually. We tried a contact lens in January of 1987, which you wore briefly, but it was too uncomfortable and you went back to wearing eyeglasses.

We utilized patching in April of 1980 to help improve your vision in the right eye, with you wearing the eyeglasses.

Things were quite stable, but by March 1989 it was evident the left eye was riding higher than the right eye. It is somewhat uncertain as to why this happened at that time in 1989, but injuries to one eye can affect the muscle balance in the other eye. We put a prism in your eyeglass to try and help resolve the double vision. There was no glaucoma. There were some lens opacities that developed from the injury slowly over the years.

As to your question whether this injury could create a post-traumatic stress syndrome (PTSD), I would say yes. As a young child, you had a significant injury, which limited your vision and disturbed your depth perception and coordination. This kind of injury also would make you shy away from contact sports, naturally, and with good reason. This could have impacted your relationship with your peers. You could not "run and play" in a normal manner as you were growing up. A reaction to this sort of scenario can vary from one person to another, but certainly it was a significant traumatic event thrust upon you at an early age. The ramifications as you grew are hard to project, but it certainly could have left its mark.

If there is any other information I can give you to help, I would be happy to do so. Best of luck with your life in Colorado and with writing your book.

Yours truly,

Dr. Richard D. Davenport

What Dr. Davenport had conveyed to me in 2015 about PTSD resulting from a traumatic physical injury was confirmed during a training I attended for work in 2019. Talking with the speaker, Dr. John Nicoletti (Ph.D., ABPP Board Certified Specialist in Police and Public Safety Psychology), I shared my eye injury experience. Dr. Nicoletti replied, "That type of early childhood trauma can definitely contribute to a PTSD reaction. You experienced a very unsettling event for a child."

• • •

At the hospital on the day of the injury, I was a trauma-ridden preschooler, so it was determined it would be best for me to be treated as an outpatient. Dr. Davenport started me on a treatment of eye ointment and patched my injured right eye. He also prescribed a sedative. The next day he saw me in my home and added an anti-inflammatory steroid.

For seven years, from 1978 to 1985, I was seen often

by Dr. Davenport for follow-up visits—the conclusions are shared in his letter above.

In January 1987, at age thirteen, I was interested in possibly trying contact lenses. I attempted to wear them for a period of time, but the lenses were not helpful—they felt uncomfortable and caused a burning sensation. My only alternative was to return to wearing eyeglasses, which I disliked. I suffered headaches when reading and after physical activity I experienced double vision. Of course, I had extraordinarily poor vision in my right eye, confirmed 20/800 without the corrective lens. My left eye distance had deteriorated to 20/50. I had to wear eyeglasses in order to see out of my injured eye and to help improve the vision in both eyes.

The injury caused a number of abnormalities in my right eye: an iris rupture, a partially dislocated and tilted lens, a scar, high myopia, probable amblyopia, and ocular motility disturbance. As a specialist, Dr. Davenport determined that these abnormalities substantiated that the changes to my right eye vision were due to the traumatic injury. His belief was that any future treatment was unlikely to change my vision loss. The physical trauma had impacted both eyes and my psyche. Thankfully, in 2014 and 2015 I was able to have eye surgery at the Eye Institute of Utah to correct my vision to 20/40 and 20/20!

When I returned to kindergarten, I was made fun of for wearing eyeglasses. I can still hear the jeering of two boys in particular. My classmates wanted to try them on to see how bad my vision was. It was no wonder my eyeglasses were found in odd places—under my bed and outside in the yard. I'd grown sick of the questions and attention my eyeglasses garnered and I often disliked being the center of attention.

Rarely wearing my eyeglasses, I became primarily dependent on my left eye.

The thought of having to wear eyeglasses for the rest of my life kept me upset because my thoughts gnawed on the fact that my injury could have been prevented. I believed I would have been a better student and athlete and my mental health more stable had I not been injured. So many times I wanted to crack my eyeglasses in half and stomp on them, but what would that prove or settle? Nothing. The injury had happened and somehow I needed to learn to accept it—that acceptance turned out to be a long time in coming. Consequently, my mind became a trap for negative images and thoughts. Even now I battle against the tendency to turn any positive into a negative.

> **Life Lesson #6:** Surviving and thriving in life have a lot to do with being mentally tough and maintaining a positive attitude.

Wearing eyeglasses in high school, I didn't want to come across as rude when my peers asked to try them on. I pretended the attention didn't bother me. It did. Most responses upon trying them on were, "Whoa! Are you *blind*?" My typical response was to play it cool. "Maybe in my right eye, but my left eye is 20/20. No big deal." But inside, it felt like a really big deal.

My anger built over the years and I had no healthy outlet. I'd often push it down and try to act calm and cool as though not at all affected by the injury or needing eyeglasses. Hiding feelings and bottling things up is extremely unhealthy. If negative emotions are not released in healthy ways, like sharing them with others, we all know what happens. The built-up pressure eventually erupts, oftentimes in spewed anger. My escalating anger became an active volcano that blew countless times.

At age nineteen I was thinking of all the future eye-injury related expenses facing me as an adult. Those would be beyond normal eye exams and sports goggles. I'd need expensive eyeglasses and I still hoped to wear contacts and to have eye surgery at some time in the future. Angry and fearing the mountainous financial burden, I filed a lawsuit against my neighbors' homeowners insurance company in hope of getting a lump sum settlement for pain and suffering. I needed the security of knowing I would be able to pay those future beyond-average expenses.

I settled out of court but was upset about the amount. I considered it too small—a molehill to the mountain of expenses I would face. I was very discouraged, but instead of saving that money I made an impulsive feel-good purchase. I bought a WaveRunner. Feeling a lack of justice in the settlement had stoked my anger further toward my neighbors, their attorneys, their insurance company, and even my own attorney. All the while, I worked to maintain a pretense of calm and cool.

Ironically, in high school many classmates thought I was such a nice guy. In truth, I felt disrespected on a number of levels and from an early age felt paranoid about others disrespecting me. My anger at God, the neighbors, others, and myself became so engorged that I envisioned standing in the street in front of the neighbors' house, a burning cigarette hanging from my mouth and a smoking AK-47 from my hand, as I shot out their windows—when nobody was home, of course. I wanted to make a point: Don't mess with me! In hindsight, I would perhaps rephrase that to "*stop* messing with me." It seemed the universe was against me and out to take me down.

The mind can erode to blackness with evil and wickedness. It can decay into mental illness, a serious and scary thing. For years I allowed my injury to hold me hostage in anger as I continued to believe the lie that my eye accident defined me as a person. How wrong I was.

> **Life Lesson #7:** You are not defined by what you've done or experienced or by what you possess or pursue.

I wouldn't come to know these freeing, life-giving truths for a very long time.

3

Sink or Swim

When I was young, anxiety caused me to vomit. That happened every time I went to swim lessons and sleepovers. I couldn't spend the night in my friend's family RV, parked in their driveway right next door, without eventually becoming ill. I had a very difficult time spending the night anywhere away from home because I felt highly insecure, feared the unknown, and experienced separation anxiety. But who doesn't want to be included and hang out at a friend's house all night? I'd go anyway, knowing what would happen.

By late evening at a sleepover, I'd feel the anxiety snaking through me about the time Ed McMahon introduced Johnny Carson on TV. While others were chugging late-night sodas, sitting and laughing on sleeping bags, I'd be in the bathroom vomiting with anxiety, my stomach feeling as if I were on a roller coaster plummeting to my death. I'd work myself up so much that vomiting was inevitable and became expected. It was the same when I'd visit my cousins overnight in Antigo, Wisconsin. I couldn't seem to avoid becoming nauseated with anxiety when staying away from home or even simply anticipating social events.

Every five to ten years I'd see an uncle who had been a straight-A student, quiet, and private. I believe anxiety kept him from pursuing the career he'd hoped for. I often wondered if I was allowing my own anxiety to keep me on the path of mediocrity, not living up to my potential and skirting too close to becoming a hermit like my uncle. I began to fear that too.

Often I dwelled on my eye injury. Doubt and fear would flood my mind as I worried excessively: Generalized Anxiety Disorder (GAD).[2] Constant worry and fear—about everything—plagued me. *What if I get a bad grade in school? Are others disappointed in me? Am I doing something socially wrong or weird? What is my bank balance? Is my boss happy with my performance?*

I rarely shared my feelings with others, out of fear of being considered weak or weird. My thinking wasn't healthy—it was dark and chaotic.

By age fifteen my anxiety had enlisted another player: severe paranoia. By age twenty, I suffered with chronic debilitating depression. I was uneducated about mental illnesses, so I couldn't see the warning signs. When I finally realized the perilous path I was on, I also saw that I wasn't alone. Millions were on the same hazardous road. My mission to change my mental and physical health and to help others began to evolve when I took steps to secure help from professionals and to educate myself about mental illnesses

---

2 "Generalized Anxiety Disorder (GAD)." *Anxiety and Depression Association of America: https://adaa.org/understanding-anxiety/generalized-anxiety-disorder-gad* (January 24, 2019).

and health—and pushed myself to make healthier choices.

Knowledge is power.

My mission grew to help others manage mental illness by prompting preventative care. Poor mental health impacts so many people, holding us hostage to negativity—the gateway to the three Ds: depression, debilitation, and disease.

The Anxiety and Depression Association of America (ADAA) wrote,

- Anxiety disorders are the most common mental illness in the U.S., affecting 40 million adults in the United States age 18 and older, or 18.1% of the population every year.
- Anxiety disorders are highly treatable, yet only 36.9% of those suffering receive treatment.[3]
- Researchers are learning that anxiety disorders run in families, and that they have a biological basis, much like allergies or diabetes and other disorders. Anxiety disorders may develop from a complex set of risk factors, including genetics, brain chemistry, personality, and life events.[4]

The ADAA also wrote,

- Approximately 8% of children and teenagers experience an anxiety disorder with most people developing symptoms before age 21.
- Only about one-third of those suffering from an

---

3 "Facts and Statistics." *Anxiety and Depression Association of America: https://adaa.org/about-adaa/press-room/facts-statistics* (January 24, 2019).

4 "What causes anxiety disorders?" *Anxiety and Depression Association of America: https://adaa.org/living-with-anxiety/ask-and-learn/faqs/what-causes-anxiety-disorders* (January 4, 2019).

anxiety disorder receive treatment, even though the disorders are highly treatable.[3]

Life Lesson #8: Know your mental and physical health. No one can take care of you like *you*.

Those of you in junior high and high school, educate yourself on mental health disorders. Don't be proud; we each have issues, every person. Those who *appear* healthy may be a mess inside and you just don't know it, so be kind to others. Because I became really good at hiding the truth and masking my feelings, people are often surprised when I share my invasive history of emotional and mental struggles. Learn from my mistakes and open up to a mature and trusted mentor. Just because someone looks as if they have it all together externally doesn't mean they are not battling internally.

I can relate to a lot of the symptoms people endure while battling serious mental illness because I suffered with extreme social anxiety, paranoia, explosive anger, and debilitating depression for far too many years. At forty-plus years old, I could count on one hand the number of serious romantic relationships I'd had: two. I wanted a wife, but I was content being single.

Paranoia increased fear in me, which fed my anxiety. When eating out, I thought all eyes were on me, that I was being watched and judged. I feared looking like a slob. I feared choking. At parties, tremendous social anxiety produced racing thoughts, a pounding heart, a shaky voice, stomach discomfort, and uneasiness—all which fed my paranoia. It was an ongoing vicious cycle. Whenever the spotlight was on me or I was simply in a group conversation, I'd freeze and internalize the moment, get a shrinking feeling, doubt myself, and want to flee.

My life began to change for the better and I became healthier when I realized the importance of thinking positively—as in, *I'm thankful I have my left eye and some vision in my right eye. I'm thankful for . . .*" There is always much to be thankful for in the midst of challenging circumstances. I needed to stop focusing on all that was wrong in my life and be present and focused on all that was right. I needed to be mindful and to immerse myself in things I really enjoyed, like reading. Most days I set aside time to read.

Back to "knowledge is power," I learned the hard way that knowledge is the pilot light that ignites the human *will* toward change—unmasking one's self, choosing the healthy road, and being dedicated to the daily maintenance necessary to avoid veering off into a ditch. In my efforts to swim rather than sink, I researched my issues and pushed myself to ask questions of professionals. Choosing to swim over sinking included becoming aware of my mental health status and my need to become more physically and socially active. I had to *choose* to get off the couch, step away from my computer, and get active and involved. Isolation isn't the answer but rather adds to the problem.

> **Life Lesson #9:** Change is a choice. We've heard this often but it bears repeating.

It did me a world of good when I got a gym membership and also chose to get outside regularly and absorb God's natural vitamin D—sunshine—and breathe in fresh air. Simply getting out, walking, and working out are keenly beneficial to mental health. Also essential are opening up to talk about feelings with trusted family, friends, and professionals and choosing a mind-set of turning worries and fears around to positive truths. Maybe the following truths should be taped to our mirrors:

- I will study/work harder and do my best.
- It doesn't matter what others may think.
- I will let go of negativity and choose the positive perspective.

Yes, all easier said than done, as I'll reveal through my poor choices, but worth pushing myself to practice with patience and persistence, swimming toward mental and emotional health and *freedom.*

Sink or swim? For a long time I was drowning.

Before diving deeper into my experiences, let me be clear: I love the people in my life *very much,* and I've come to forgive as I hope others will forgive me. I've ruined many relationships that I need to repair.

No matter who has hurt you or wronged you, no matter how poorly you've behaved, forgiving others and yourself is mandatory for your healing and wholeness. Genuine love and the way we display love are also of utmost importance. I no longer want to sulk and say *woe is me,* blame others for my anger and unhealthy mental health, or have a pity party and call myself a victim.

There came a time when I was faced with the choice to address the elephant in the room—my own mental health condition—and the choice to begin loving and forgiving others and myself. But that road was a long journey.

4 Countdown to Insanity

1986–1987

Like many, I had a dysfunctional childhood and made attempts to protect those I loved. I'm still very protective of my loved ones. In hindsight, as an adult I see that I handled such situations poorly.

> **Life Lesson #10**: Dysfunction in one's youth can cause undue emotional stress on a child. Poor choices and responses by adults perpetuate unhealthy cycles from one generation to the next.

Adults: We're each responsible for our own decisions and actions, which include the examples we exhibit to children. We must practice relationships through a heart of genuine love, eyes of empathy and truth, feet of forgiveness (walking out forgiveness), and hands of practical helping. For starters, we must seek out

> mature people to share our feelings with, and at times we must talk with a trained counselor.

I was a troublemaker in middle school. I stole, fought, rebelled, didn't listen, and didn't care. I was often in the principal's office. While I may have caused a lot of trouble, I had a blast doing it. I hung out with the cool kids and had fun. My best friend was a classmate and we had some good times, especially at his home after school in the winter. We threw snowballs at passing cars, road his ATV in his wooded backyard, and blasted heavy metal (Motley Crue) from the radio. I needed an outlet for my anger issues and that was doing the trick.

Around that time, I started becoming interested in girls and inappropriate books and magazines. Impure thoughts were running rampant in my mind.

> *Parents*: Be aware of what your kids are looking at and listening to (print, video, and audio). The mind can quickly become warped.

Many youth have become confused about their sexual identities and genders because homosexuality has become accepted and even pushed by society to public policy that calls it "natural." This saddens me because this mind-set is contrary to the Word of God.

I believe a lot of gender confusion occurs when a child is brought up in either an unstable environment (such as addiction, divorce, parent's death), an unnatural environment (like same-sex parenting), and other unhealthy environments (as in poor marriage relationship, abuse, secular views, lack of principles and morals). By God's perfect design, boys are created to be attracted to girls as girls are created to be attracted to boys.

Foremost, let's remember that the gay community is full of hurting people who are no worse sinners than heterosexuals.

• • •

During a football game in 1987 at a neighborhood school, I got into a fight with my good friend. The other boys took his side. I don't recall what led to the disagreement, but I was physically threatened by the other boys—to the point that I transferred to another school. This event fed my anger and my fight-or-flight mentality. I fled externally and fought internally. That was the year I began to spiral into the pit of OCD. I became even more shy and introverted. My life experiences had drawn me into doubting myself and taught me to bottle up my emotions instead of freeing them in healthy ways.

The OCD started with me counting things. First the stairsteps at home and then at school. To this day I count. I count while shaving and showering and drive myself crazy as I count my way into insanity. I was not aware in junior high that I was in the early stages of OCD. In order to feel safe at home, my compulsion was to count to five—my favorite number.

I'd begun to lay out my clothes for the next day in the exact order I would get dressed. I didn't care about homework, but I sure was orderly. Even my backpack and locker stayed neat and tidy. My surroundings and everything I did had to look and feel perfect, everything in its place and tidy at all times.

The OCD had me doing nightly walkthroughs of our home from the basement to my bedroom as I counted.

Just a few examples:

- Bathroom and kitchen faucets had to be securely off.
- Toilet seats had to be down.
- Toilet seats had to be wiped down three times after every use and counters wiped down five times—perfectly clean.
- Hand towels had to hang perfectly on the racks.
- Hangers in my bedroom closet had to be plastic and the same color, white; no wire hangers allowed.
- Closet doors had to be shut.

1, 2, 3, 4, 5

- Refrigerated goods had to be checked often for expiration dates.
- Stove had to be off.
- VHS tapes and files in the filing cabinet had to be alphabetized.
- LEGOs had to be organized by color and all toys perfectly ordered.
- Paint cans in the basement had to be organized so labels were facing front and visible.
- Nails and screws in the carpentry room had to be in their designated drawers—no mixing and matching.
- Light bulbs had to be snug and tight in their sockets.

1, 2, 3, 4, 5

- Doors and windows had to be closed and locked.
- Cabinets and drawers had to be closed securely.
- Blinds had to be drawn at the same height during the day and at night pulled all the way down.
- All windows had to be opened at the same height or all closed and locked.
- Toothpaste had to be squeezed perfectly from the bottom.
- Rugs had to be squared.
- Light switches had to be touched to ensure they were off.
- Products on counters had to be perfectly arranged.

1, 2, 3, 4, 5

- Junk drawer had to be organized.
- Clothes in the main closet had to be sorted and ordered by person, season, and size.
- Cushions and pillows had to be plush on the couches.
- Dishwasher had to be loaded and unloaded a certain way.
- Clean silverware and dishes had to be put away just right.

And here were my car checks.

- Car doors had to be locked at all times, whether I was in the car or not.
- Seat belt had to feel snug.

- Gas tank had to be full.
- Trunk had to be checked to make sure it was closed.
- Radio station presets had to be in ascending order.
- Parking brake had to be on when the car was parked.

And so on. *1, 2, 3, 4, 5.* I also reread whatever I had just read. I felt I had to read the local newspaper before I read the national newspaper, and I had to read their sections like this: front page, other sections in a particular order, and finally sports—saving the best for last. When I did not follow those strict compulsions, I'd experience anxiety and stomach pain.

What's more, all my checking, counting, ordering, and cleaning had to be done in silence to avoid detection by others. I didn't want anyone to discover my obsessions and compulsions. I suffered in silence as millions of others do. If there was disorder anywhere, with anything at any time, I'd have stomach discomfort. Likewise, following through with all the infinitesimal tasks created stomach distress because the list was endless, time consuming, and the final result had to look and feel perfect to me.

I knew enough to recognize that such behavior was not normal or healthy, but, again, I didn't know anything about obsessive-compulsive disorder. I lived in constant fear and anxiety that something bad or disastrous would happen if I failed to check each and every thing every day.

At night, after checking the entire house for any imperfections, I would try to lie in bed perfectly: sleeping on my back in the middle of my bed, hands folded across my chest, staring directly at the ceiling fan. Then I would try to think and breathe perfectly. And I'd assure myself by saying,

"Everything is okay because everything is perfect."

In truth, my world was far from perfect. A dark force of obsession and compulsion drove me all day, every day, in all things.

• • •

Despite my lack of interest in schoolwork, I was a good speller and actually wanted to compete in spelling bees. But because of fear and anxiety, I didn't. My life is full of regrets, but I now know it's *not too late* for me to accomplish many of my goals. Those just won't include spelling bees.

> **Life Lesson #12:** Wherever you are in life, no matter your age, don't let fear hinder you from pursuing your goals and dreams.

At age thirteen (1987), I discovered painful lumps in my chest that eventually led to surgery (1994). The diagnosis was the hormone imbalance *gynecomastia*. The growths led some kids to refer to me in an unkind term. Kids can be mean, stealing self-esteem. Between my eye injury and the need to wear eyeglasses with a thick lens, a dysfunctional youth, the OCD, and gynecomastia, my confidence was shot and my emotions were growing hotter.

> *Parents*: Be good role models so your children will learn their own value and the value of treating others with kindness and respect. Be actively invested but avoid overcontrolling their lives. Good values start in the home with an emotionally healthy dad and mom who work to balance appropriate discipline with empowering love.

1988–1992

In high school I continued to struggle with mental health issues. Further anxiety and anger fed apathy. These were made worse when two seniors, much bigger than I was, would chase me down the hallway. I was a 130-pound freshman and their prop for proving to others how tough and cool they thought they were. But it was scary for me. I can still picture those guys, and the memory triggers anger. When I saw one of them fifteen plus years later at a high school baseball game, I seriously considered confronting him. I wanted to ask, "Do you remember chasing me in the hallway? Do you think you're so tough now? Let's throw down." As hard as it was to maintain self-control, I chose the high road and said nothing. I sure did want to approach him. I wanted revenge; I wanted to win.

That high school incident brings to mind the person who ridiculed me at a football game thirty years ago. I still struggle with the desire to get revenge, but I recognize that I must continue to choose forgiveness and let it go. Easier said than done, but forgiveness and taking the high road are mandatory for those who truly desire to gain and maintain mental and emotional health.

> *Parents and teachers*: Bullies should be taught at home and school to understand the demeaning and debilitating effects their cruel behaviors have on their victims.

I just wanted to survive high school and somehow graduate. Overall, I was not a very good student academically. My A grades stood for anxiety, anger, and apathy. Fighting these demons left little energy and motivation to focus on things that didn't come naturally for me—like math and basketball. I was a 2.252 student, ranked at 130 out of 203—

but my locker was always neat! It took a lot less energy (and was more quieting, safe, and enjoyable) to sit and watch sports on TV at home. Sports was my go-to, my safe place, my energy booster. I'd skip classes to go home to watch college basketball games and hardly ever missed an NFL game, which also proved at times to be an outlet for my pressurized anger. When the Packers lost to the Vikings in 1994, I punched a hole in the wall. Not a healthy outlet. Thankfully my hand did not find a stud.

> **Life Lesson #13**: Perpetually living in survival mode consumes the mental energy needed to achieve responsibilities and the things that don't come naturally to us.

I really struggled with math and didn't care for algebra or geometry, which were required to graduate. It's funny that I had a relative who taught math and several who were accountants, but I didn't inherit the math gene (or basketball gene). I adopted the defensive mind-set that math served no purpose so I didn't need to learn it. I went to summer school for math between my junior and senior years, and because of geometry I almost didn't participate in high school graduation or play summer baseball. Gratefully, I somehow graduated and was allowed to play ball that summer.

When my classmates talked about their college plans, I felt worthless and inferior. But looking back, I wouldn't change a thing. I now understand that college isn't for everyone. College is only *one* of several ways to discover one's natural and unique gifts, preferences, and purposes.

> **Life Lesson #14**: We're each wired uniquely to fulfill a different purpose.

For those who know what they want to do after high school, a college degree may be their road map. For others, a college degree may bring only temporary happiness in the workforce, and they soon find themselves back at square one and carrying a heavy weight of debt. Too many college graduates are enslaved to debt for years. For those struggling with battered mental and emotional health, college may feel overwhelming and unmanageable. There are many scenarios. Thank God there are several viable paths to learning and succeeding in life. One can look into enrolling at a trade school, joining the military, or simply just working.

5
Losing is Unacceptable

In my sophomore year, I wrote the following English paper (I added the italicized phrases later).

English 11-01
8/31/1990
Paul

I am sixteen years old and the middle child. I love watching and playing almost every sport: baseball, football, basketball, tennis, and hockey. I also enjoy playing golf, bowling, badminton, ping-pong, and darts. I work at Milwaukee County Stadium, ushering at Brewers' baseball games and Green Bay Packers' football games when they come to town.

The thing I like best about myself is my kindness and *ability to get along with others.* I don't often get upset unless I dislike someone who gets on my nerves. Those people are usually loud and obnoxious. I'm easy to get along with once you know me.

> The thing I like least about myself is my *lack of confidence.* I don't have too much confidence in my school work or sports, mainly basketball. I also dislike that I have *a bad temper,* which I rarely display *unless I'm very upset* with someone or something.
>
> More than anything, *I want to be successful in life at everything I do.* That includes school, sports, and my career. I want to accomplish many things in life and hope I do. I'd like to go to a small college and play on their baseball team. After that, I'll go on from there.

Let's break this paper down.

First, as far as my ability to get along with others, I tried so hard for so long to get people to like me; I was a people pleaser. I'd let people walk over me until my suppressed anger would erupt.

> **Life Lesson #15:** Trying to please others only makes you dislike yourself and steers you off course from your unique God-created purposes.

Second, my lack of confidence in high school wasn't apparent to others but it was to me. And my bad temper was the result of bottling my emotions and not releasing my anger in healthy ways. So between the two, I imprisoned myself from living a fully engaged life in my teen years and well into adulthood.

Finally, I wanted (and still do) to be successful in life at everything I do. The truth is that the "road to success" (college), as I viewed it through the lens of my poor mental and emotional health, felt like enormous added pressure, which ignited a flight response in me.

> **Life Lesson #16:** Life is full of ups and downs, successes and failures. In sports there are always a winner and loser, but that won't matter in a hundred years. The important thing is to find a healthy balance and maintain a positive mind-set. Simply do your best at whatever you're doing and embrace failure as an opportunity to learn and improve.

We all fail, and that's okay. The greatest failure lies in not flipping that coin to its positive side: those who fail at something are those who are actually getting up and trying—giving their best within their unique circumstances. Getting up and giving your best *is* success. The many times I did get up and gave my best in high school and after, I couldn't see those efforts as the true successes they were. I didn't realize back then that everything we set our hands to is a learning experience that grows us in some way. And I didn't know that God doesn't waste a single second of our time or experiences.

I played baseball in high school and regretted that I didn't also play football. I considered myself too thin for football. I was afraid of getting hurt, and I had an excuse not to play and therefore not fail. But for two years I played tennis.

I was slated to be paired with a friend to play No. 1 doubles on our varsity tennis team, but I felt it would be too much pressure on me. I avoided failure by simply not playing. Choosing to be undetermined was easier. My poor mind-set was *I can't fail if I don't play.* That's a bad attitude to have about sports and anything in life. What I would give now to say I had met that challenge and played. Lesson learned in hindsight. I encourage everyone in junior high and high school to avoid regrets by playing whatever sport you enjoy or are curious about. Heck, try them all and any area of interest—school clubs and other extracurricular opportunities. What's the worst that can happen? You'll lose a tennis match or basketball game that no one will remember. The best that can happen is not a trophy or a slew of ribbons but that you got out there and *lived life*; you did your best while playing and competing with your friends in something you enjoy.

• • •

Tears of anger and disappointment stung me when I was cut from the eighth-grade basketball team. I lacked confidence to be the best player I could be. But in high school, I got back in there and played. I earned the nickname Ogg, which has stuck over the years. I was a thin, lanky white male who resembled Alan Ogg, the University of Alabama-Birmingham basketball player who also wore Rec Specs.

I started at center on the freshman B team (what a cast of characters!) and also in my sophomore year on the JV team. In my junior year I rode the pine, as they say (bench). As I shared earlier, I was missing the basketball gene, but I was sticking it out. All the while, I suffered severe social anxiety during warmups. Questions plagued my thoughts to the point that I couldn't focus. *What if I miss a layup or miss a shot in the pregame? Will rude things be yelled out at me from the bleachers? Will I hear about it the next day at school?* Being on the basketball court was mentally exhausting for me, even in pregame. By outward appearance I was very timid, but deep down I was angry, anxious, and afraid—and trying to keep those emotions hidden. The persistent anxiety and fear of failure provoked more anger in me and all three trauma responses: fight, flight, and freeze—a vicious cycle of mental illness. For one varsity game, I was so confident

I wouldn't get to play that I wore nothing but underwear under my warm-up suit. For good measure, I should have also ordered a pizza to be delivered to the bench. I was that confident in my lack of confidence.

One month into my senior year, the anxiety won and I gave in to the flight response and quit the basketball team. I didn't share with anyone that anxiety was the factor. I should have. At the time, it felt easier to quit—another decision I came to regret. Hindsight being 20/20, I see not only my regrets clearly but more importantly I see how God is using my poor past decisions to help me and others make good present decisions. I tell high school students to stick it out! Who cares if you sit the bench or miss a shot? Remember it's *just a game*! Gripping this truth with a mind-set of determination to enjoy yourself will empower you to step up and play your favorite sport or try some other activity you're interested in. If not sports, maybe join the math club or try out for that part in the school play. Whatever your interest, don't miss the opportunity to get in the game of life and enjoy that time with your friends!

> **Life Lesson #17:** You can't get this time in your life back, so make the most of every day.

While I "played" basketball for three years, baseball was my passion and still is. I was an all-star every year from grades one through eight, and I was a starter on the freshman, JV, and varsity baseball teams. Playing baseball was a lot of fun. My senior year of baseball was the most fun I've ever had playing any organized sport. Our coach was fiery and energetic, a man who had won three Wisconsin state high school baseball titles, so he knew what he was doing. He was a terrific coach and I have great memories of him. I wrote the following letter in 2015 to support his induction into the Greendale High School Hall of Fame.

> I am writing to you in favor of my Varsity high school baseball coach being inducted into the Greendale High School (GHS) Coach Hall of Fame. He coached GHS baseball for 20 years and has an impressive overall record of 375-226 (a .602 winning percentage). He's a family man, a man of character, a great teacher and baseball coach who knows the game well.
>
> More importantly than baseball knowledge, however, he taught the valuable life lessons of leadership, handling adversity, passion, integrity, and character to his ballplayers. He is a good role model and a winner.
>
> Lastly, he was inducted into the Wisconsin Baseball Coaches Association (WBCA) Hall of Fame in 2009. I think this humble man, in my opinion, is highly deserving of this award/nomination.

During senior year, Coach was looking for a right fielder and I volunteered even though I had no desire to play outfield. In my junior year I was the team's No. 1 starting pitcher and assumed I'd have the same role in my senior year. I'm not much of a risk taker, but I decided to give right field a shot. It was a combination of fun and anxiety. My friend played center field. He was a stud athlete, so I had some peace of mind having him next to me. Thank you to my buddy, Number 2 in center field!

My first time out, Coach called me "the natural." Looking back, I should have been called "the head case" as anxiety ruled my thoughts. *Will I see the ball off the bat? What if I misjudge the ball? What if I don't make the catch or I make a bad throw back to infield?* For a game I so love, I didn't enjoy being in the moment as much as I could have. That's regretful. I was too worried about failing as a right fielder to enjoy the experience. But for some reason, when I occasionally played center or left, I felt comfortable. Bizarre.

As it turned out, I was an all-conference honorable mention utility player my senior year. However, instead of enjoying that success, I was upset that I wasn't an all-conference choice, having batted close to .400 and hitting well my senior year. For years, when the subject would come up, I'd share that I was an all-conference baseball player and leave out the "honorable mention" because I cared too much about what others might think of me.

I coached kids' baseball in Colorado for eight years. A lot of fun. I often thought I had more fun than the kids did when I hit fungoes to them and pitched batting practice. I still experience tremendous social anxiety when coaching, but I'm determined not to give up or give in. I'm determined to get up, get out, and give my best.

> **Life Lesson #18:** Determination is a steel mind-set of choice—ideally toward things that are good and healthy.

Not a single incident of our lives is wasted—good or bad. Not wanting to waste my struggles, maybe one of my purposes is to help boys grow into good, healthy, loving men.

Attitude goes a long way toward achieving success or failure. I urge you to picture success and understand that what's considered a success for one person is not necessarily a success for another. But a mind-set of losing is unacceptable. When a mistake is made—which will happen—*who cares?* The human element of sports is what makes the moments so great! We're not robots; we're human beings who succeed at times and fail at times. It's all part of the game and life.

6

"To Steal and Kill and Destroy"

Two natures beat within my breast.
The one is foul, the one is blessed.
The one I love, the one I hate.
The one I feed will dominate.
—Anonymous

Throughout high school I pretended to be calm and cool. I was everything but. I was paranoid and hypervigilant, worried about the smallest and biggest things. During lunch it was *Who's watching me eat? Do I look like a slob? Are there crumbs on my face?*

During my junior year, a friend and I thought it would be a good idea to blow something up. I was rebellious and angry, looking for an outlet and that adrenaline rush that masks as living. Obviously, a poor decision and dangerous act. I'd share the details of the crime, but I don't want to plant bad ideas in young readers' minds. I don't know how we managed to avoid arrest. The police were all over the scene with their K-9s and flashlights as we escaped the area and went to see a movie, *The Silence of the Lambs*.

Jesus said about Satan, "The thief comes only to steal and kill and destroy" (John 10:10). A key way he accomplishes this is through our minds. The mind is where it all begins—every thought that leads to a decision and action. Mental health issues are serious at any age and can lead to awful decisions and tragic outcomes, but there is good news. Jesus continued in John 10:10, "I have come that they may have life, and have it to the full." How? Learning and practicing God's principles. So many young people are struggling with anxiety, anger, and depression, and many lack healthy ways to express these negative mind-sets.

Mental health concerns need to be addressed with young people, not simply to avoid their derailment in adulthood but also to give them an opportunity in youth to live life "to the full" and to continue that health into adulthood! The responsibility to teach God's principles and stay attuned to the emotional and mental health of children and teens rests on the shoulders of adults—parents, relatives, teachers, coaches, church communities—which makes it essential that adults keep themselves in good health in every way by living according to God's principles.

I was also a liar in high school. I chose to drive to a fast-food joint that required a stint on the highway. My two good friends, Jason Freitag and Jon Olsen, and I initially told others we were going to a malt shop in town. I was sixteen or seventeen and didn't want anyone worrying about me driving on the highway, so I lied about our destination. I hid the truth out of fear of getting in trouble and fear of others judging me. I must say that Taco Bell meal was delicious!

Life Lesson #19: Lies will one day be found out. Telling the truth is much easier and certainly wiser.

My parents went out of town for a week during my senior year, and when one's parents go out of town, other classmates find out and hop on the opportunity. I had told a few people at school I'd be home alone for a week, and of course word spread like wildfire. I was at home playing pool with my two good friends when I heard a knock at the front door. Peeking out the darkened windows, I saw some popular "cool" kids standing on my porch. I hadn't wanted them there so I had taken precautions by keeping the house dark, expecting that some would show up with alcohol. I didn't answer the door, just continued shooting pool, and they left. But they returned a little while later.

I called the police in hope that a simple drive-by would convince the kids to leave. I didn't want them drinking at my house and then driving home intoxicated. The police said they'd drive by. As it turned out, they pulled up and got out, and my classmates ran. It was obvious to them that someone had called the police. I hadn't wanted that kind of police response; I had simply wanted the group to be scared enough by a drive-by to leave. That idea sure backfired, but perhaps that call saved a life.

The following Monday in school, the group of cool kids confronted me with name calling. I can still hear one guy jeering, "Calling da PO-lice!" I was furious at the police for not simply driving by as they'd said they'd do, and I was upset with myself, feeling mortified and thinking I should have just let my classmates into my house. Peer pressure is no fun and very real.

> *Kids*: Don't allow yourself to feel bad for doing what's right, regardless of what others think or how they react. By the way, those popular kids who seem cool today often have serious issues as adults. Just because someone seems cool in the moment doesn't indemnify them from their own mental health issues that lead to adult addictions, unemployment, and jail. Playing cool (as I did) is often a mask that popular kids wear to cover their uncool issues. If you're not one of the popular or cool kids, this moment will pass, so hang in there and do the right thing!

I had no idea what I was going to do after high school. I often thought about going into the military, but I had too much anxiety and was essentially blind in my right eye. Instead, I followed the masses and attended a two-year university for a semester. Not surprisingly, I still had very little interest in school and a lot of need to vent.

One day while driving to campus with friends, a vehicle cut me off in traffic. I wanted to follow the driver and confront him, but, thankfully, my friends' cooler heads again prevailed and we went to class. (Thank you both for talking me out of following that vehicle!)

On another occasion at the university, I was given a parking citation that really upset me. Because I disliked authority, I decided to pay the citation in pennies. I can still picture sitting on my bed at home in Greendale and counting those coppers. I dropped off the citation with a sack full of coins and walked away. This is not a brag but an emphasis on my unruliness. So many times I wish I could go back to high school and be a better student and athlete. I also wanted the girls to like me and for the anxiety to be taken from my youth. I wanted a do-over at home, in school, and with sports.

> *Parents*: I highly encourage you to get your children involved in sports for the innumerable benefits. Let them play multiple sports. Don't be overprotective. Sports can teach children to be humble winners, good losers, and team players, and they'll learn the value of hustle, good sportsmanship, and respect for others—including authority.
>
> *Kids*: Set aside your fears and play any sport that interests you. A lot of life is simply showing up, whether for school, work, or sports. Don't be like me, having regrets many years later.

In 1993, having temporarily thrown in the college towel, I moved to Vail, Colorado, where I had family. I lived there about four months and worked full time as a crew member at a fast-food joint and part time as a busboy at a café. The fast-food joint afforded me cheap employee housing and the café a free ski pass. I don't know what I was thinking; I was working sixty hours a week and had little time to ski.

Burnout followed pretty quickly. Coupled with my simmering anger and dislike for authority, I had moments of stubbornness with management. I was exhausted and wasn't having fun. One day I slept from midnight until six in the evening—eighteen hours.

I had no idea what to do with my life in my late teens, but here's another fact: You can take the boy out of the state, but you can't take the state-of-mind out of the boy. Running to Vail was not the answer to my issues.

My sister, Michelle, and her friends were drinking age, but I wasn't, so while they were out, I stayed in my apartment and watched sports. I had a roommate who was as thin as a toothpick and quite the character! He claimed he was a ninja and was wanted by the Asian mafia. He sure was entertaining.

One day at work, he claimed he had to leave the premises as the Asian mafia had just come in for lunch. Good times we had!

While working in Vail, I didn't want to listen to anyone; I wanted to do my own thing. I continued to nurture my negative mind-set. *How dare you tell me what to do! I am my own person, and I'll do as I please.* Or so I thought. I found out the hard way that this mentality doesn't fly in the business world. I was repeatedly called into the manager's office at the fast-food joint. I failed to show up for work at the café one day, thinking, *They don't appreciate me. I'll show them.* I thought I might be terminated, but I didn't care. I missed Milwaukee and wanted to move back home.

Four months in Vail was enough for that nineteen-year-old with a very bad attitude. *It's time to go back home and do something with my young life,* I told myself. For those of you still pondering what to do with your life, find your passion. Money will come with time so don't do something that makes you dread going to work or makes you miserable. Working is a good thing, a necessity, so find your passion and stick with it. Mind-set: one day at a time.

I moved back to Milwaukee, leaving my sister, Michelle, who is my best friend.

Now what?

I had dreamed of becoming a police officer or working for the FBI; I thought these were manly things to do. Unfortunately, many police officers and agents get divorced and have substance abuse issues. None of us are immune to life's struggles and difficulties. We often think others don't have issues, but they do—including our pastors. We're each human first and foremost.

I thought being a police officer would give me the respect

I felt I had lacked growing up. I felt inferior and worthless but enrolled at a technical college to study police science. Again, I was an average student (2.7344 GPA) who cared more about getting through the day and watching sports than studying and getting good grades. I dreaded having to give the required oral class presentations. You know how it's said that one would rather die than speak publicly? I agree. I presented on a police subject and was angered and humiliated when the instructor asked questions and critiqued my presentation in front of the class. From the silence of my thoughts, I was screaming at him, *How dare you ask me questions! You aren't even a police officer!* My heart was racing, my face was turning red, and I wanted to run out of the room.

The difference between my inward hostility and outward calm came from so badly wanting to be liked and respected. I cared so much about what other people thought. I briefly tried out for the college baseball team only to quit because of anxiety. I was afraid others in my life would be disappointed if they learned I'd quit the team, so I pretended all season that I was playing. Caring too much what others might be thinking was a detriment to my wellbeing. I didn't share with anyone the battles taking place in my mind. Don't make the mistakes I made. Talk to a trusted and mature adult in your life; be real and honest.

After getting my two-year degree in police science, I looked for employment, though not strictly in law enforcement. The procrastinator in me wanted to put off working in the real world because the real world seemed intimidating, especially to someone with extreme social anxiety.

But how could I postpone the real world?

7

"All the Jobs My Uncle Has Had"

My niece, Kiley, contributed the title for this chapter because I changed jobs thirty-four times in the span of three decades. I was a mess, and here's my resume to prove it.

1990–1993: Midwest Services (at Milwaukee County Stadium)

At age sixteen, I'd noticed a peer from high school working at Milwaukee Brewers baseball games. What could be better than a baseball fanatic (me) working at professional baseball games? I applied for a job, was interviewed in a group setting (yes, I experienced severe anxiety), and was hired as an usher. Right off the bat (pun intended!), when reporting to work, I got lost in the stadium. I sprinted from the lower level to the bleachers, unsure where I was supposed to be. As it turned out, I made some good friends I still keep in touch with. It was a fun job taking tickets, ushering people to their seats, and answering fans' questions. And I saw some altercations in the bleachers. Best of all, I was able to watch a lot of baseball while getting paid. The work was a good experience, but my anxiety was intense.

1993: Wendy's and Mid-Vail Café

Various times I was called into the manager's office at Wendy's, where he told me I needed to improve my attitude. The day after a verbal confrontation with my supervisor at the Mid-Vail Café, I didn't show up for work and he came looking for me at Wendy's. I hid in the back while he talked with my manager there. I was upset that he'd shown up and that I was being talked about. I disliked the negative attention and the authority.

1993: Play Outlet USA

Upon returning to Milwaukee from Colorado, I worked as a stocker at the sporting goods store. I wasn't there long; a fellow coworker complained often about an injury (a broken pinky) I had sustained playing quarterback in backyard football. Apparently, I was not productive enough for him. Between his complaining about my bad attitude and injury, I was compelled to quit.

1994: 440th Airlift Wing Airforce Reserve Unit

My next stop was at age twenty at the Air Force reserve base in Milwaukee, working as a civilian in the role of Morale, Welfare, and Recreation Attendant. During that time, I was taking classes in police science at Milwaukee Area Technical College (MATC). Both were working out fairly well, considering my challenges. On the base, I checked people into the recreation center, provided customer service, and washed towels and cleaned bathrooms. The cafeteria offered sandwiches and delicious carrot cake that I'd help myself to after the staff left. The downside? I felt that cleaning toilets was way beneath me. I was proud and stubborn.

An aspect of the job that incited tremendous anxiety in me was making military ID cards. Something about people watching me do *anything* caused me anxiety and doubt, which led to anger and wanting to go off on people. When anyone watched me make an ID, I'd want to yell, "What are you looking at?" I thought I was a mind reader, believing they were thinking, *Does this man have any clue what he's doing?* The perpetual lies streaming through my mind led to even more anger.

Once when I was trying to say something to a coworker, I totally mumbled and he made fun of me. Embarrassment seized me as I asked myself, *What was that?* I don't know what caused the mumbling, but from then on I'd often struggle with articulating words and overall verbal communication. It was bizarre. I suspect that incident may have heightened the severity of my social anxiety and dread of social situations. Nonetheless, I needed to work to eat and have a roof over my head.

1995: The Grand Milwaukee Hotel

The largest hotel in Milwaukee, near the airport, offered me a job as a security officer. At this point, I was dating a girl and had an apartment and roommate in Greenfield, Wisconsin. The job was a good experience, but my anxiety level skyrocketed whenever I had to deal with guests and coworkers. I tried to look and act like a tough guy, but inside I was struggling. I had panic attacks but hid them well. I'd work late and hang out until four or five in the morning with coworkers, which would provoke so much anxiety in me that

I often thought I'd vomit.

1995–1998: Marquette University

A friend told me that Marquette University had job openings for full-time third shift as a residence hall officer—checking IDs and other such security efforts. This could potentially lead to a public safety officer position. A lieutenant in the Department of Public Safety said in a group setting, "Paul is PSO material." He was referring to me potentially becoming a public safety officer. I still had zero confidence in myself and was very uncomfortable with his proclamation, not wanting such public attention or the expectations that felt like pressure to perform.

My interest was piqued when I heard that university employees received tuition assistance. I applied and got the job. As a full-time employee, I received seven free credits per semester. I enrolled for nine and paid for the additional two. This is a great way to pay for college tuition and avoid getting deep into college debt!

My classes were toward a bachelor's degree. For three years I attended classes during the day and worked from 11:00 p.m. to 7:00 a.m. It was a healthier and more stable period in my life—even though the social anxiety persisted and I lacked sleep.

I still have nightmares that I'm not going to graduate from college. I recall receiving notices in the mail about failing grades during my first semester at MU. Anxiety had me holding on to my high school mentality: just show up, be organized, listen, and move on. But that minimalist thinking didn't fly at the university level. To succeed, I had to mentally *commit* to asking questions, completing extra-credit work, seeking tutors when needed (not surprisingly for math), and actually *studying* the class material. I didn't want to fail. I was very competitive, so I began to see my degree work as a challenge and mission to earn a college degree from a prestigious university—in part to impress others because earning a degree would, I hoped, cease the lies I carried in my head that others viewed me as stupid.

The experience taught me the importance of being prompt, reliable, hard-working, and dedicated to a goal. In May 1999, I graduated with a degree in Criminology and Law Studies.

My only regret was not pursuing school further to earn a master's degree. I realize it's not too late. I'd still like to reach that goal, but I wonder if this desire is more about impressing others rather than gaining knowledge that would potentially offer me a higher quality of life in a career I enjoy.

> **Life Lesson #20:** Let go of caring what others think! Find your passion and pursue it!

1998: UPS

Working as a truck loader was fast paced, which sent me rocketing into higher anxiety. In my head I'd scream, *I don't need you and all your boxes!* Not long into this job, I quit. From a payphone, I called in sick and said, "I won't be in . . . ever!" I too often lived in flight mode, but each job was a tool that honed for me a clearer understanding of what work and environments were best suited for my passions and my mental health.

> **Life Lesson #21:** Countless varieties of work are either compatible to your unique wiring and will encourage your mental health . . . or outside your

wiring and will incite greater distress and illness. Don't stay stuck; stay busy learning who you were created to be and what jobs are best suited to your uniqueness. Not only will you be happier but so will others in your life.

1999: New Concept Self Development Center, Inc.

After graduating from Marquette, I briefly worked as a youth mentor for a juvenile justice organization in a very rough neighborhood in Milwaukee. As one of maybe two white people working there, I was paranoid that my black coworkers would think I was racist. The lies in my head, including being nervous about being the only white male, wouldn't stop. I felt trapped and debilitated. In truth, my coworkers and employer were very nice. I was there maybe three months when I decided to return to the field of greatest longtime interest, police work.

2000: Milwaukee Area Technical College, Police Recruit School

Ten weeks in police recruit school earned my state certificate as a police officer in Wisconsin. *What was I thinking?* At police recruit school, recruits learn the ins and outs of policing. Though I had long been a competitive person, I would grow very defensive, anxious, and angry while competing in recruit school. I honestly don't know how, with my mental health issues, I made it through the training.

We took turns at roll call when we had to ensure all recruits were in attendance and share a motivational quote. When it was my day, I shared this Japanese proverb: "Fall down seven times, stand up eight." Someone made a negative comment in response and I wanted to get in his face and ask,

"What's the problem?"

During a week of firearms training I had a huge fear of doing something wrong and getting yelled at. I would look left and count to five, and then I'd look right and count to five. The OCD aspect of my thinking constantly steered me toward perfectionism. One instructor actually told me, "You look like a robot." I felt like one! I had a robotic mentality from trying to be perfect and from fear I wouldn't be. I feared I would accidentally shoot a classmate or instructor.

One day I was shaking from nervousness and the firearms instructor pulled me aside and asked, "What's going on? What's wrong with you today?" I tried to be calm and cool though I was anything but. I replied, "I'm rather new to handling firearms and I guess maybe a little nervous." The insecurities I was tangled in pushed me to want to ask him, "Do you think you're better than me?" We went back to the shooting range and I somehow got through the day. I was a survivor and my motto was "survive the day!"

> **Life Lesson #22:** One day at a time, one moment at a time, one prayer at a time, and sometimes one breath at a time. Break down the bigger picture that overwhelms you and practice pursuing the smaller, more manageable steps.

2000–2002: Strong Funds

Still dodging the real world as a police officer, I applied for a job at Strong Funds as security. I had a lot of fun. I learned about the opening through someone who was working there and encouraged me to apply. I was twenty-six and had finally learned how to use email.

After the first year, the familiar need to flee crept over

me and I interviewed for a position in account services. In the interview, I was asked some computer-related questions and in answer I made things up. I was good at that. I got the job. Being a perfectionist, I was awarded several times for zero-error work, which encouraged me. But a few times an error was called by the quality assurance team—I took those times very hard and personally instead of seeing them as opportunities to learn and grow. After about a year, I looked for another move within the company and landed a role in quality assurance. That work was a lot of fun and I met some good people. The position was a good fit for me, but after a time I began to grow paranoid that management wanted me to be more productive.

My thinking continued to sabotage my life.

2003–2004: Northwestern Mutual

Early in 2003, I made a regretful mistake when I chose to leave Strong Funds to try my hand at sales for this large insurance company in Milwaukee. It was a numbers-driven role and I don't do well in positions that require a fast and demanding pace. I prefer to take my time to ensure my work is done right—or rather, perfectly.

During training in the position as a financial representative, a trainer asked me, "Are you normally so mellow?" I didn't know how to respond. It was common for me to hide my emotions. Here's the pre-hire evaluation I found:

> Paul M. Gallagher (2003)
>
> Overall, I think he is going to require time, effort, energy and attention on the part of a Supervisor and rigid adherence to our programs, without which I don't think he will make it.

> Emotionally his feelings are mildly responsive to other people and they are consistent. They are very deep and he is able to make an emotional commitment; they are not always spontaneous which means it begs the question whether or not he can put people at ease on contact. He may need to be taught to issue approval without requiring approval in return.
>
> He is emotionally stable, not emotionally outgoing by nature.
>
> In the area of mental processes, he is thorough, logical and pays attention to detail. His concentration level is above average. He is able to think in an organized pattern. He shows imagination. He will benefit from training sales technique and rigid adherence to your program is imperative. Functionally his goals are security oriented. His self-motivation is precise rather than dynamic and aggressive.
>
> His determination and ability to stay with what is undertaken is good and it is that, that I am depending on that he will stick with your program. He is aided in his efforts to achieve by imagination, organizational ability, pride and self-reliance.
>
> In the area of social fear: he has a strong desire for certainty. I think he fits into a corporate structure a lot better than fitting into a job where he is dependent exclusively on personal power. In the area of defenses; I don't identify any major hostility characteristics. 75%+ high side of average.

I was hired and worked on commission in a sales role. I was expected to phone prospective clients daily beginning at 8:00 a.m., meet with three potential clients a day, and dictate on a Dictaphone, all of which caused me a lot of anxiety! *How do I sound? Do I make sense? Do I sound foolish? Is the office assistant laughing at me and sharing my audio tape with others in the office?*

I shared an office with two other sales reps, and when phoning prospective clients, I felt like I was having a panic attack. It's an awful feeling, as if someone is standing on my chest. I don't know how I managed, but I was a survivor. I'm surprised now that I lasted more than a week at this job.

When I attended sales training in downtown Milwaukee, I thought I was going to vomit. Prior to entering, I had sat in my car for a while, not wanting to go in. I had searched out the garbage can in the room and also knew where to find the restroom in the event my fear became reality. My anxiety made me think I had an ulcer. I had kept a heating pad on my stomach to help with the pain, but it didn't work.

Anxiety was taking a physical toll on me. I had gained significant weight. I had bruxism—grinding my teeth while sleeping, which wears off the enamel. I suffered with tension headaches, stomach and chest pains, and shaking-leg syndrome. I was a nervous wreck. I kept asking God, "When will this end? Father, please take this from me."

During this difficult time, I'd go days without bathing or brushing my teeth, and I wanted to die. I often stayed home instead of going to work. I just didn't care. I had no energy.

A coworker, upon learning about my depression, said, "Just snap out of it, Paul." I learned that it doesn't take the snap of a finger. Mental health is a journey that requires attention to every aspect of one's lifestyle: physical, mental, emotional, and spiritual.

Again, I thought I knew what my employer was thinking about me, and I thought I was going to get fired. I panicked, left the company, and entered counseling. More on counseling later.

2004: State Farm Insurance

I had decided to work hard at this job to learn everything I could about the insurance industry. As a customer service sales rep, I would be the first contact with customers, so the downside of this job was, again, my extreme anxiety. Greeting the public was nerve-racking. I quit after two months and would soon be participating in OCD treatment.

2004: P.M. Bedroom Gallery

For one month I worked at the furniture warehouse. I didn't want to socialize with coworkers because of my heightened anxiety. As an escape from social interaction, I worked alone, breaking up boxes. A mere four weeks had passed when I exchanged words with a supervisor and quit. Out of anger, I took legal action against the company and was awarded $1,000 for not having received "a reasonable accommodation" to attend OCD treatment. I found that I enjoyed playing attorney (at my computer) because that official role allowed me to tell people in authority not to bother me—and playing attorney made me feel intelligent, which is what I wanted others to think. I was thirty-one and still I despised authority.

2005: UMB Fund Services

As a phone rep speaking with strangers and filtering through their needs and questions, I lasted only two and a half weeks; the position was a bad fit. I dreaded being on the phone with friends and I'd taken a job being on the phone as a salesman. While shadowing other phone reps, my thoughts ridiculed me. *What am I doing here? I don't want to be here.*

What do I say? How do I say it? Do I sound rude? What if I don't know the answer to a question? How can I handle questions from strangers?

I had to get out of there. I fled yet again.

2005: Kanavas Landscape Management

What could be more mentally and emotionally relaxing than making mulch deliveries? I thought.

My supervisor had an issue with the time it took me to make deliveries and shared his concern with me. Of course, anytime I felt threatened or unappreciated, my tendency was to go off on people, especially those in authority. My defensive thinking was, *I'm going to take my sweet time in making my deliveries, and if there's confrontation when I return, so be it.* The second time the owner discussed my performance and the concerns of my supervisor with me was in his office with my supervisor. Angry, I wanted to get in the supervisor's face. But I didn't; I just quit on the spot.

2005: Oconomowoc Developmental Training Center

Serious mental health issues continued to plague me, and I left the role of youth counselor after a few months. I should have been one of the patients rather than an employee.

2006: CS Logistics, Inc.

Working as a courier required a vehicle and I used my own. I enjoyed the independence of the job but disliked the necessity of dealing with people. I was still in therapy, under the care of a counselor and doctor, and I took a brief leave of absence. I received a prescription for anxiety and then returned to work. But the anxiety was persistently severe, and I fled the job.

2006: Milwaukee School of Engineering

Because of extreme anxiety, I almost didn't last a day as a public safety officer. On the night I decided to quit, I was driving to work for third shift and knew I had to work with someone who wasn't popular in the department. On a downtown street, I took a right instead of the left that would get me to work and I headed back home. My thoughts were incredulous. *Am I really doing this again? When will this anxiety and misery end? Will I ever hold down a job long term?* The debilitating anxiety felt like a vice crushing my head and like someone stomping on my stomach. This job at MSOE could have been a career with the job description and expectations, the pay, the benefits, the people, the schedule. But it just wasn't the right time.

Sidebar: Steve Barry wrote this in his article, "4 Illustrations of What Anxiety Really Feels Like":

> Chronic anxiety is messy and unpredictable, overpowering and insidious, physical and mental, and at times so unexpectedly debilitating I'm unable to speak or think clearly or even move.
>
> Like a knife stabbing you in the chest with each breath you take
>
> Like a rain cloud of negative speak following your every move
>
> Like an impostor hijacked your normal self
>
> Like an explosion in your brain, sending your thoughts spiraling out of control[5]

---

5 Steve Barry, "4 Illustrations of What Anxiety Really Feels Like," August 26, 2019, *Healthline: https://www.healthline.com/health/mental-health/what-anxiety-looks-like#10* (January 20, 2020).

2006: Henry Logistics, Kelly Services (at U.S. Bank), Midwest Express

I delivered medical supplies throughout Wisconsin and put such tremendous pressure on myself that I became physically ill anticipating failure. My anxiety was such that I quit after a week.

I'd had so many different jobs by age thirty-three, I can't recall exactly when I worked for the temp agency, but two assignments were at banks. Although I'd interview well (and often), I'd draw blanks at times during the interviews and tremble when responding to questions. Because I didn't have a stable work history, I'd lie my way through. Interviewing was an unpleasant experience for me. My mental illness was severe.

For several days I worked security for an airline and was again debilitated by anxiety and paranoia. My health was declining in every way.

2007: Elite Human Capital Group (at Northwestern Mutual)

On a temporary contract to set up new accounts, I returned to the insurance company I'd worked for between 2003 and 2004. On the morning of my return, I was so ridden with anxiety and stomach pain that I almost didn't go in. I had awakened early in anticipation. Many early mornings thereafter, I was in my bathroom sick with dread and anxiety before going to work. I was sure to carry plastic bags with me on the bus (Milwaukee County Transit System) in case I vomited. My job included filing papers in an office filled with phone reps, and that environment caused me such chest pain at times that I thought I was near a heart attack.

Anxiety was preventing me from sleeping well at night,

and depression was preventing me from gaining rest when attempting naps. Riddled with such severe anxiety, I wanted to walk off of that job too, but somehow I managed to make it through the nine-month contract.

When the contract was up, some temporary employees were offered full-time roles at the company. As I tended to have issues with authority, especially women, I wasn't offered a job. This really upset me. I thought I was being treated poorly and being singled out for lack of production due to my OCD. Angry thoughts battered me. *I have a college degree! I worked as a financial representative for this company! I'm very detail-oriented and own a life insurance policy with this company! So this company owes me a job!*

Unable to express my feelings well, I was also very defensive. While discussing with my female supervisor my future with the company, I was fully in the fight-or-flight mentality. I wanted to call her every name in the book while simultaneously wanting to simply go home.

After I was let go, I collected unemployment for the first time. I could have easily stayed on unemployment, along with disability and food stamps, but I was too proud and stubborn to ask for assistance and take from taxpayers, so I continued to job hunt.

2008: Waukesha County Alcohol Treatment Court

As a counselor for the court, I had to share an office with a coworker. Sharing space with someone felt more threatening to me than working alone. I continued to feel that others were judging me and looking down on me. These perpetual lies in my head were triggers that fed my anger and anxiety.

The treatment center was a court system organization that met with individuals who had multiple DUIs (driving under the influence). As a counselor, I naturally had to meet with the offenders, which terrified me. I recall sitting in the parking lot on my first day of employment, feeling panicked and thinking, *I can't do this!* I texted trusted people to pray for me. Because of my personal drinking history, I also felt hypocritical. I had long feared being arrested, which tied into my dislike of authority and fear of losing control. At that time, I didn't see my job as a way to help others because I was blinded by paranoia and fear, thinking others were judging my every move.

During my brief time at this job, Michelle and I met for lunch at a Wendy's. I was so full of anger and anxiety that I threatened to throw a chair through the window of the restaurant, which was my way of saying nonverbally to the world, *Nobody messes with me! I'll put you through a window too for judging me!* I didn't act on my thoughts, but I was sure tempted to throw that chair. I knew right from wrong, which helped me maintain a level of self-control, thankfully. I had no doubt I'd be in prison if I didn't exercise self-control.

Just weeks after beginning this job, I quit. I can still picture sitting at McDonald's in Franklin, Wisconsin, feeling that I was a loser, I couldn't hold a job, life was not worth living. . . . *Now what? Is there any hope?* I felt I was at a dead end in life. *What's going on with me?! How long will this extreme anxiety be the ruling force over me? Should I be institutionalized?* I desperately wanted peace of mind. During lunch with Michelle, I asked her, "How long will this last? If we come back here in a year, will anything in my life have changed?"

I'm so thankful for Michelle, my trusted best friend. After a counseling session, I met her in Whitnall Park, a place very special to me where I found peace walking and reading in nature. I opened up to her about my issues and broke down and cried. Had she not been in my life in 2008, I may not have made it. Talking with her gave me a sliver of renewed hope and I was able to say, "There is hope."

I played in an annual stickball tournament in Greendale, Wisconsin, for many years. Such group activities significantly raised my social anxiety to a higher level—the competition, other men, socializing, winning or losing. I was often picked toward the end of the draft, which also pricked at my low self-esteem. Teams were drafted by captains and being picked close to last both upset me and motivated me. I often had a chip on my shoulder. *Here we go again. I'm being underestimated.* Looking back, as with much of my life, I wish I had enjoyed the moment. I didn't. I couldn't. In ten years of playing in the annual stickball tournament, my team won five Doweler Trophies. No big deal.

As imperfect as my life was, I would one day look back and see the purpose for my pain. The reasons would be revealed as part of my perfectly imperfect walk. Michelle was there for a reason, in part to encourage me as I battled intensive mental illness at the lowest of my lows. She took the time to write out prayer cards to encourage me:

> Lord, Your Word says, "Oh Lord my God, I called to You for help and you healed me" (Psalm 30:2). Deliver Paul from anger, depression, and anxiety. Do not let these emotions rule over him. Anoint him with the "oil of joy" (Isaiah 61:3), refresh him with Your Spirit and set him free from negative emotions this day.
>
> "For troubles without number surround me; my sins have overtaken me, and I cannot see. They are more than the hairs of my head, and my heart fails within me" (Psalm 40:11–12). Oh Father, this is how Paul feels now. "Come quickly, Lord, to help." Be his "help" and "deliverer" and "do not delay" (Psalm 40:13–17).

> Lord, open Paul's eyes so that he can see what you want him to do for work. Lead him and assure him that you have uniquely gifted him with ability and talent. Help him to know that you have "great and unsearchable things" (Jeremiah 33:3) waiting for him. Reveal this to Paul and open doors of opportunity which no man can shut. Your Word says, "Let the beauty of the Lord our God be upon us, and establish the work of our hands for us" (Psalm 90:17).
>
> Lord, I pray your Holy Spirit would guard Paul's mouth so that he will speak only words that bring life. Your precious Word says, "Put away perversity from your mouth, keep corrupt talk far from your lips" (Proverbs 4:24). Help him keep his mouth godly. Fill him with Your love so that out of the overflow of his heart will come words that are "pleasing in Your sight" (Psalm 19:14).[6]

Thank God that she cared enough to walk with me and help me through my ordeal.

6 Michelle paraphrased many of these Bible verses.

> **Life Lesson #23:** A healthy support system will help you through the difficult times. Anyone can be there when times are good, but who will be there when times are bad? Surround yourself with mature believers in Jesus who will pray over you and encourage you through the bad times and rejoice with you in the good times.

2008: Steinhafels

My bad attitude followed me into this job as well. I was working as a delivery associate and wanted to fight my male coworkers. In my head was the same defiant question I wanted to scream aloud: *Do you think you're tougher or better than me?*

Fear ruled me. It was out of the fear of looking foolish in front of others that I didn't want to learn how to pack a truck of furniture. I would push the furniture to the rear of the truck for loading but avoid everything having to do with actually loading it. Not surprisingly, I gave in to the resounding lies in my head and stopped showing up for work.

2008: JMX Same Day Delivery, LLC

As a courier for this Milwaukee company, I made deliveries throughout southeastern Wisconsin and northern Illinois. I traveled to Chicago often. Contending with the bad traffic caused me chest pains. By that time in my life, chest pains were part of my daily battle.

2009–2011: Medspeed, LLC (subsidiary of Aurora Health Care)

I worked for this company for three years. It was a great fit my first year. I drove alone, over 300 miles per night throughout Wisconsin, delivering medical supplies, pharmaceuticals, and such. I was independent and I loved it. When I was almost hit head-on by a driver who may have been under the influence of alcohol, I was thankful I hadn't been distracted with the radio or anything else or I could have been killed. After that incident, I asked for a route in the Milwaukee area and continued to battle my demons as I worked.

Things ended poorly at work when I felt unappreciated and disrespected over a quarterly bonus I'd earned but hadn't received. I was a believer in Jesus but not bearing the fruit of His Spirit. I wrote a letter containing some regrettable statements to my supervisors and others in management. Going off on people was how I lived. I knew I needed help and needed to change, but I hung on to my anger and rebellion. I went out for a going-away party on December 16 and didn't go in to work the next day—my way of rebelling against the company for withholding the bonus. Again I played attorney and eventually received the money I'd earned.

In late 2011, I moved back to Colorado and worked solely on this book for about three months before my next job.

Sidebar: In February of 2012, my niece and I were on a national radio show discussing climate change. Before going on air, I drank several shots of tequila. *I could barely hold a conversation with my dog when he was alive, so how can I possibly go on a radio show where tens of thousands of people will be listening?*

2012–2013: Cordillera Metro District and Go Rentals

On the job for a little over a year as a public safety officer, I started to realize I could indeed hold a job for more than a week or a month—a groundbreaking realization. I met some good people there despite my anxiety, self-doubt, and anger issues.

I wanted to work more than thirty hours a week, so I took a job at the car rental agency in the county airport. I thought I'd found a good job, but the anxiety came roaring back full force as I shadowed my supervisor for two weeks and then went to Scottsdale, Arizona, for additional sales training. The moment I walked into the training room and was introduced to everyone, the chest pains, racing thoughts, and stomach discomfort hit me. We were seated in a circle, which I absolutely dread even to this day, and were expected to give sales presentations in front of the group. I was extremely anxious and wanted to tell everyone off because I thought they were judging and mocking me. Yes, my attitude was awful.

Part of training involved driving expensive vehicles around the neighborhood, and I wanted to crash the one I was driving to say, *Nobody messes with me or judges me!* My mind was a mess. I wanted out.

I packed that night and looked at the bus and train schedules. I would have walked across the country if I'd had to. While my coworkers were meeting at the training site the next morning, I was checking out of the hotel. The owner of the rental company had given us each a bag of goods and I handed mine to the front desk clerk and asked her to give it to the company owner when he returned that evening. I was paranoid about what the hotel staff might think of me leaving the training early: *Why is this man leaving? Is he a failure?*

Out of paranoia and embarrassment for jumping ship, I said to the clerk, "There's a better job offer on the table back home." I took a $304.80 flight back to Denver, still believing all the lies in my head.

In an email to management, I apologized and shared the truth about my longtime and debilitating anxiety and the panic attacks over having to give group presentations and participate in role playing. I explained I was overly uncomfortable in group settings and having chest pains. And I shared the fact that I was on medication.

I was back to square one—again—which felt like jail. "Do not pass go. Do not collect $200."

2013: SkyWest Airlines

I worked for the four-month ski season at the county airport, loading and unloading aircraft while continuing to battle tremendous social anxiety. I believed I was being watched and judged by coworkers and passengers. It was mentally exhausting, but I stuck it out for the season. I often wonder how I survived working anywhere at that level of anxiety and paranoia! I didn't want to be like that, and somewhere inside me I knew God had a greater purpose in all the pain. I told myself to simply keep putting one foot in front of the other and trust Him.

2013: The Ritz-Carlton

I worked as a loss prevention officer for the hotel and experienced a lot of anxiety there as well and actively fought against the lies in my mind. I worked at the hotel for almost a year when I decided to accept employment doing manual labor. It was more money, closer to home, and the job allowed me to coach baseball on a more consistent basis. Plus, I'm more of a blue-collar kind of guy. I don't care to be clean shaven and all dressed up. Give me steel-toed boots and blue jeans over a suit and tie any day of the week.

2014: American Gypsum Plant

I worked as a utility operator at the plant. Besides sweeping and cleaning the plant floor, I did lawn care, snow removal, trash disposal. Part of this job also involved handyman duties such as painting, lawn care, and hanging pictures. I felt confident in this role, though I was by no means a handyman! Funny story, I was asked to hang pictures outside the main office area. They had no clue that I wasn't handy. The pictures ended up crooked and looked awful! My friend there had to help me.

I had a confrontation of sorts with a coworker who worked in shipping and receiving. He was unfriendly and I was very stand-offish toward him. I would occasionally cover his role when he was sick or on vacation. While he was on vacation one week, I took a can of Mountain Dew from his office refrigerator and emailed him that I took one (wanting to be honest and transparent). When he returned, he made the incident a big deal, blowing it way out of proportion. He and I just didn't get along; we were both proud and stubborn, coupled with being insecure and defensive.

Being left alone for the most part, I was overall somewhat at peace. I had my own little handyman office where I'd work, play music, and read. I had made friends with some of the men and actually enjoyed the role until I began to care too much about what two of my other coworkers—a woman and Mountain Dew incident man—thought of me. The fight-or-flight mentality kicked in and I fled.

2014: ECO Transit

I washed and cleaned buses, fueled them, and did basic maintenance like oil and fluid checks. This job didn't last long because of my issues with authority—surprise, surprise! I lasted maybe three months, thinking I was too good to be washing and fueling buses. *Pride!*

2015-2018: Vail Health

My duties were in purchasing for two years, involving a lot of counting, numbers, and computer work, which increased my anxiety. I was also pulling cases for surgeries and my OCD kicked in as I didn't want to make a mistake and look incompetent. That stress and the need for particular hours to coach baseball led me to seek the flexibility that came with working as a concierge and valet. Initially I had anxiety, but over time in those ensuing two years, I became comfortable and confident, and I met some really good people.

2019: Vail Police Department

After all those years, I finally found my career at age forty-four. The interview process took many months, including a background check, but I was offered a position as a code enforcement officer with the Town of Vail Police Department. My role requires talking on the police radio and at times I feel I mumble or freeze up. During the five-week training period, anxiety became intense to the point that I thought about leaving this role and going back to the comfort I enjoyed at the hospital. But I got through my anxieties; I've never given up. I'm too competitive and too proud to give in.

I'm grateful to be settled into this career and for the excellent benefits. I truly enjoy what I do! I have a ton of respect for those in the department and this work is a good fit with my interests, my graduate majors in Police Science and Criminology and Law Studies, and my previous training at Police Recruit School in Milwaukee.

• • •

It's clear why I left so many jobs; my mental health was very poor, causing me to continually seek confrontation and expect difficulty. I didn't know what "normal" was and I constantly and unknowingly sought what I knew best: chaos and drama. In counterbalance, I looked for opportunities and reasons to flee, thinking the grass was greener on the other side. Now I can adhere more fully to the wisdom spoken by Saint Francis de Sales (1567–1622): "Bloom where you're planted."

For those of you struggling with anxiety in the workplace, hang in there. It's not easy but stick with it. The worst-case scenario is that your employer terminates you and for a time you may need to collect unemployment. Someone once encouraged me to go on Social Security Disability because of the qualifying anxiety issue, but I was too proud to take that route; I was capable of working and seeking to find the right fit for me.

> **Life Lesson #24:** Look for work that is fitting to the way you're uniquely wired. Don't settle.

While I wish I had stayed longer at some places of employment, the truth is that I learned a great deal with each change. It was important that I kept putting myself out there, moving forward while striving to do my best under the pressure of severe social anxiety.

I urge you to make the most of every day and every opportunity because we don't get do-overs. What we do get are new opportunities and new compassions every morning through the incomprehensible love of our Creator

(Lamentations 3:22–23). Don't throw those invaluable treasures away. I didn't know these truths back then when they would have made such a huge difference in me.

We can do this.

"Do You Think You're Better than Me?"

The chip on my shoulder was a boulder of Everest proportion.

The first time I became intoxicated was with some high school friends. We had just graduated and wanted to celebrate. I was eighteen and we were on a camping trip at Lake Geneva, Wisconsin. It's hard to believe that some of my classmates had started drinking in seventh grade!

> *Parents*: Be aware of your children's friends and your children's whereabouts. Be involved in your children's lives, but don't be overwhelming or overbearing. Helicopter parents get a bad rap for a reason!

I felt pretty loose and carefree after the first few beers, which is drastically different from how I felt when sober. That false sense of freedom was the hook that snared me into excessive drinking, reeling me deeper into emotional darkness. As the alcohol settled into my system, I became uptight, serious, defensive, angry, paranoid, and anxious: a deadly cocktail. We were at a campsite and I leaned back too far in my chair and fell backward. That was rather humorous!

The second time I became intoxicated was at age nineteen at a high school classmate's home. I danced that night, which I rarely do (I really should stick with non-dancing activities)! After vomiting in the bathroom, from alcohol rather than anxiety, I was asked to leave the party, and a friend drove me home. I probably thought I was cool at the time. The truth is, I was not in control of myself—the alcohol was. I ended up briefly sleeping in my front yard and then somehow made it to the bathroom floor, vomiting and sleeping next to the toilet. The next day when my parents asked what had happened, I defaulted to my habit of lying and claimed I'd smoked a cigar and gotten sick. They didn't buy that weak excuse nor should they have. I'm living proof of this life lesson:

> **Life Lesson #25:** Nothing good comes from intoxication with alcohol or drugs. These inflate the struggles we battle when sober. And nothing good ever comes from lying.

At age twenty, I went to a party in West Allis, Wisconsin, with two friends. We were looking forward to watching Pearl Jam on *Saturday Night Live* when a man changed the channel just as they were about to appear. He and I exchanged words. He said I was arrogant, and we almost came to fisticuffs. We were separated but not before fear grew an apple-size lump in my throat as I faced fight-or-flight. Luckily, my two friends were able to get us out of there safely.

For my twenty-first birthday, my friends and I went to Madison, Wisconsin, for a party. My birthday happens to be on New Year's Eve—the big party night, of course. Since

I had turned twenty-one that day, I purchased a keg and had several beers. The alcohol coursing through me was a matchstick that struck my paranoia and lit my deep-seated anger. I wanted to fight someone.

I was wearing my favorite Milwaukee Bucks baseball cap and heard a man at a party say in mockery, "the guy in the Bucks cap." Immediately, through the lens of my paranoia, I was enraged that he was talking facetiously about me. Thankfully, my friends intervened and peacefully resolved the situation.

For me, excessive drinking is like entering the ring to fight myself—and pulling others in to fight me. I was already confrontational when sober and had a long history of fight-or-flight responses. From behind beer cans and shot glasses, the same question taunted and triggered me about others. *Do you think you're better than me?* That mentality of paranoia and confrontation was at the root of all my anger and the ensuing years of poor choices. I really believed that others thought they were better than me and were out to prove that. I was out to prove them wrong by exercising my brawn.

• • •

The death of my grandfather (Felix Preboske) in 1994 sent me spiraling into grief and further depression. He was respected and feared and represented all the manly qualities I desired. He was a teacher, hunter, fisherman, outdoorsman, and a football and basketball coach. He'd played college basketball and was captain of the 1935 Wisconsin Big Ten Championship team (I have the necklace). He went on to play for the Oshkosh All-Stars, a professional basketball team. You can read more about him at www.probasketballencyclopedia.com.

Grandpa was a smoker (died from lung cancer). He

sported a tough-guy persona with a hard exterior. I aspired to be like him, but I often felt inferior and worthless. I chose to roll with fighting and playing the tough guy to mask my true feelings.

Shortly after my grandfather's death I visited some friends at their college. I got intoxicated and ended up angry at a restaurant. Battling grief and hanging on to anger, I wanted to start a fight. What was I thinking? In my friend's apartment, I tried to knock over his refrigerator and would have succeeded had he not intervened.

> **Life Lesson #26:** Anger is a God-created emotion and at times justified. The key is how we choose to use our anger. It can be productive or destructive.

A friend who was attending a Wisconsin college invited me to visit him and take in a college football game. Because of severe anticipatory anxiety, I made an excuse and didn't go, but I did visit him a few weeks later. I would regret that visit. We were going to a college party and the mere thought of attending a social event ramped up my anxiety. Once we were there, I became so anxious I headed outside and vomited. To cover my embarrassment from those passing by, I played it cool and murmured, "I'm hammered." I wasn't; I was struggling with severe social anxiety.

A key player on the insidious team of social anxiety is paranoia. Mixed with aged anger and alcohol, paranoia produces a cocktail of violence and self-harm. The paranoia I battled when sober morphed into pandemonium inside me when I was intoxicated, erupting in molten rage onto others.

At age twenty-five, in the spring of 1999, I attended a softball tournament in Greendale and traveled Water Street in downtown Milwaukee. Drinking, I ended up in a street brawl that could have gotten really ugly. Some young men were picking on a friend of mine who was developmentally delayed. Being a protector, I couldn't stand by and let that injustice happen. The alcohol gave me a false sense of bravado and I told the man picking on my friend that he was in the wrong. He didn't like what I had to say, and we started throwing drunken punches. Those fifteen seconds felt like a half hour. Fighting was not what I wanted to do, but the pendulum of my mental illness swung between fight and flight.

The next thing I knew, I was against a fence taking punches from three men. A friend intervened and knocked the smallest man out of the picture while another friend laid punches into the instigator. My friends really took care of business that night and I believe their use of anger on behalf of our defenseless friend was justified. That left me and the remaining guy, but I was so intoxicated I can't recall what happened next—only that the police arrived and that was that.

A year later I was in Chicago for a bachelor party in 2000. I'd driven down from Milwaukee with some friends. Because of my severe social anxiety, I tended to disappear at social events. My disappearing acts earned me the nickname *Houdini* by my friends. I have countless Houdini stories—just ask! In this particular story, I left the establishment about midnight and wanted to take the train home but found that it wasn't leaving until the next morning. I flagged a cab and asked to be driven to Milwaukee. The driver thought I was kidding. I wasn't. He got approval from his supervisor and off to Milwaukee we headed. I sat in the front with him and we had a great conversation. One hundred thirty-five dollars later, I was back home.

On Saint Patrick's Day in 2001, friends and I were again bar hopping along Water Street. Police were directing traffic due to the high volume of people on the streets and sidewalks. Of course, I was tipsy and feeling feisty. We were crossing the street when the pedestrian signal changed to *Don't Walk*. An officer told us to turn around. Incredulous, I spouted, "Are you serious? We're halfway to the other side!"

"You heard me!" Pointing, he shouted, "Turn back." I threw an obscenity at him and found out very quickly that police do not care to be sworn at or disrespected. Two officers escorted me to a squad car, where I was identified, questioned, and (fortunately) released with a verbal warning.

I'd often had issues with authority—law enforcement, teachers, coaches, umpires, bosses. While sober, I disrespected a softball umpire when he called me out at second base after my head-first dive. Looking back, I see that I was rude and mean, both immature responses. There was no reason for me to call the umpire names. I should have been kicked out of the game after my tirade. Such behavior against authority is not justified.

> **Life Lesson #27:** We may not agree with authority, but we need to respect it and show good sportsmanship. We need to respect everyone: teammates, coaches, opposing players, officials, fans, family, friends, and strangers. Take the high road.

A few months later, same story; different day. My lifestyle oozed agitation and confrontation from every pore of my decaying mental health. I was at an Independence Day party in downtown Milwaukee and, yes, I'd had a few beers too many and became aggressive. I'd been talking with a woman whose brother was also at the party and he apparently told my friends he didn't like me talking to his sister. I confronted the whole lot of them—the brother, his friends, and my two friends—and snapped with belligerence, "What's the problem?" Choice words were exchanged, followed by me pushing two guys against the porch rail where I asked again, through clenched teeth, "Is there a problem here?"

Nothing good comes from intoxication. I hadn't figured that out.

That August, after playing a softball game in Muskego, a friend and I decided to get a late meal. We'd just won first place in the league and I wanted to celebrate at our sponsor's bar with my closest companions: beer and shots. As the night wound down, we played a joke on a teammate that ended badly. Feelings were hurt and emotions rose between him and my friend. As we were leaving, the guy hurled at him, "Get lost!" My friend and I headed to an all-night restaurant without him.

Sometime later he walked in, still angry. Having fun, I feigned hiding in the booth. When a loud bang hit the table, I jumped up and saw that he was holding an aluminum baseball bat, clearly out for revenge against my friend. I went for the bat and wrestled him for it. As the bat clanged to the floor a waitress yelled, "I'm calling 911!"

Our teammate stormed out the door, but I couldn't let it go. I had taken the confrontation personally because my nature is to protect those I love, and I was peeved at the guy. I followed him outside, confronted him, and again wrestled him. He was a tough rugby player—I hadn't thought that through. I threw a few ineffective haymakers and thought he was going down when we heard sirens. Police—a couple of squad cars, a K-9 unit, a Suburban, and other unmarked vehicles—arrived in force. They took statements from witnesses and arrested our teammate.

Intoxication and misused anger are destructive. I had considered the teammate a good friend and that incident ended our friendship. I still wasn't seeing (or I was ignoring) the flashing red lights about my ill mental health. Bottom line, instead of addressing my issues head on, I kept them numbed with alcohol. Intoxication filled me with a false sense of confidence and power, which always backfired by triggering more paranoia, anger, and aggression. What a mess I was.

In February 2003, I was out with friends at a college basketball game. We'd rented a limo so we could party afterward without the hassles of driving and parking. We had a great time until I'd consumed too much alcohol. For starters, I was flirting with a married woman from high school and her husband didn't take kindly to that, naturally. Somehow squeezing out of that one, I asked the limo driver to take me back to my friend's condo where I was staying the night. It was after midnight, so I presumed he'd be there. He wasn't and I couldn't get in, which upset me. It was winter and I was freezing, intoxicated, and fuming.

I went across the street to a restaurant to wait it out and sometime later walked back to the condo. No one was there. I let fury lead and knocked the door down with my shoulder (another bad move), collapsed on the couch, and fell asleep. When my friend's roommate returned to find the door on the floor, of course that led to heated words. In the end, my foolish choices cost me four hundred dollars to replace the door and, worse, cost me another friendship.

That summer while playing in a Friday night softball league in Menomonee Falls, I got punched in the face by a woman. Apparently at a party the previous year, I'd had a few too many beers and had acted arrogant toward her, which had offended her. She hadn't forgotten and I had no excuse. I couldn't even remember the incident. The truth was, I used arrogance like I used alcohol—to mask my countless insecurities. Those strategies weren't working so well for me, but I wasn't yet seeing that truth.

I desperately needed a mature mentor in my life.

After the softball game while I was socializing in the parking lot, a woman made several rude comments within earshot behind my back. I was the kind of guy who lived in a slow simmer of resentment, saying nothing when provoked until the pressure of my irritation boiled into roiling rage. She punched me, and then I called her and her friends a few choice names and challenged their significant others to a fight. Unsatisfied, after the game I drove around the parking lot taunting them.

In 2006, I attended two weddings. After the first one, I made the potentially fatal choice to drive home intoxicated. Although I made it home safely without causing harm to others, that was a seriously foolish gamble. I take responsibility for all the poor decisions I've made through the years. No one forced me to drink and drive; no one forced me to drink and fight. Those were my choices.

At the second wedding, I felt disrespected when a man made a false accusation against me. I again let my anger control me and threatened to throw him through a car windshield. I should have ignored him and taken the high road. The high road is where eagles soar, but I didn't yet know that beauty and freedom. I was thirty-two and continuing to play the part of the vulture and victim—a hot-headed competitor plagued by paranoia and rage, always scavenging for confrontation.

In 2007, I played on a Greendale softball team. A team we didn't get along with would often make rude comments from the dugout. I'd simmer in silence, saying nothing as I played catcher while my anger gradually inflated. Once I exchanged words with a batter, and he taunted, "What? You gonna beat me up?"

"I'm thinking about it," I shot back. The question that bullied me from behind the plate was the same question that had bullied me from my youth: *Do you think you're better than me?* Whether drinking or not, I allowed my emotions to keep me on edge and on the lookout for release. Instead I should have been looking for the psychological and spiritual help I desperately needed, along with a mature mentor.

> *Readers of all ages*: If you're battling mental and emotional pain, find a mature mentor. If you're healthy, be a mentor.

After that game I jumped into another confrontation in the parking lot. An opposing player called someone on my team a crass name and my teammate got in the man's face. Always ready for a fight, I spouted, "If he touches you, I'll knock him out!" I truly thought the opposing player believed he was better than me. Cooler heads prevailed. Mine, however, remained in a steady simmer.

> *People*: We need to stay calm, be calm, practice calm. Nothing good comes from a hot head. Let it go and take the high road.

There are more examples of how my poor mental health kept me in anxiety, paranoia, quick anger, and depression. Deep inside, I wanted justice for all the bad things I had experienced as a child, but justice continued to allude me while paranoia mocked me from center stage. I was always worried that others were judging me and talking bad about me, and I'd get aggressive whether drinking or sober, whether driving or playing sports.

When I was visiting my grandmother (Lorraine Preboske) in Merrill, Wisconsin, in 2009, a friend asked me if I wanted to go to a Brewers-Twins baseball game in Minneapolis. I felt guilty about the thought of leaving my grandmother for the night, but I was also challenging myself to be spontaneous, something I rarely did. His friend had two tickets and a hotel reservation that he and his wife couldn't use, so we had a free game and free room waiting for us. Off we went to Minneapolis.

We spent time downtown before and after the game. He and I struck up a conversation with a gentleman who seemed friendly, but the more he drank the more aggressive he became. Sound familiar? It became apparent to me that he was attracted to men, and in my intoxicated state he appeared to be flirting with my friend. That set me off. I was too inebriated to remember how the incident ended, but I was told that I grabbed the guy by the neck, threw him against the wall, and threatened to rough him up. I ditched my friend in the parking garage stairwell and searched out a place to sleep in the garage. I do recall it was a miserably cold night in that concave of concrete. Although I was heavily intoxicated, I woke up often through that night, shivering. About five in the morning, I made my way back to the hotel room, where I slept until checkout time. Then I returned to my grandmother's, where I felt absolutely miserable from the alcohol and experienced freefall into severe depression. I wanted to die.

> **Life Lesson #28:** Overconsumption of alcohol and mixing beer and liquor are not wise or godly

because we lose our self-control. We're called by our Creator to maintain self-control in order to protect and preserve our minds, bodies, and spirits. We're called to honor God with our bodies, which includes our mental and emotional health.

Now, years later, having come to understand and acknowledge my mental health concerns, I rarely drink. When I do choose to drink, I enforce my limit. I've learned that self-control is a learned behavior, a diligent choice to keep one's self in control rather than allowing circumstances and substances to control. Excessive alcohol punctuates my paranoia, ignites my anger, and pulls me deeper into depression. American Addiction Centers wrote the following in "About Drinking and Depression."

> Some people drink alcohol in an attempt to cope with their depression. People can be drawn to the sedative effects of alcohol as a kind of medication, helping to distract from persistent feelings of sadness.
>
> While alcohol may temporarily relieve some of the symptoms of depression, it ultimately serves to worsen depression on a long-term basis. Alcohol abuse brings with it a bevy of negative effects on virtually every aspect of life. As a person begins to experience financial and career consequences as a result of alcohol abuse, and their relationships begin to suffer, their depression worsens. This often leads to a damaging cycle of abusing alcohol in an effort to self-medicate symptoms of depression, and the depression worsening due to the continued alcohol abuse.[7]

---

7 Edited by Meredith Watkins, MA, MFT, "Can Alcohol Induce Depression?" November 26, 2018. *American Addiction Centers: https://americanaddictioncenters.org/alcoholism-treatment/depression* (January 6, 2019).

I've driven intoxicated more times than I care to admit, and those experiences taught me that intoxication is selfish, dangerous, unnecessary, and potentially fatal. If you're planning to drink, or there's a chance you'll find liquor in hand, make wise choices in advance: a designated driver, a taxi, a sober friend, a relative—whatever it takes to avoid driving after drinking. Keep a taxi service number in your phone, just in case. I would rather spend forty dollars on a taxi than risk an accident, arrest, fatality, or prison sentence.

I know two former alcoholics. One chose to daily decrease his alcohol consumption and the other chose to go cold turkey, addressing his personal issues head-on, including no longer fleeing from his criminal past. I'm very happy for both of them. After my long battle with intoxication, the healthy balance for me is to limit alcohol. I'm all for having a beer or two from time to time, but it's simply not worth it for me to get intoxicated because I become highly destructive. I not only behave badly to others as a drunk but also tend to grow more paranoid and fall deeper into depression—sinking instead of swimming.

> **Life Lesson #29:** When we give up control of our minds and bodies to foreign substances, we make poor decisions. That's a fact. Know your alcohol limit. Self-control is key and drunkenness is foolishness.

Kids: Drinking is *not* cool!

Whether a person is addicted or not, excessive alcohol and doing drugs will lead to mental, emotional, physical, and spiritual self-destruction and relationship destruction. Please learn from my poor choices emphasized throughout this book in the patterns I repeated.

I was blackout drunk twice in my life. One time was in Minneapolis, Minnesota—the incident I shared earlier when I ended up sleeping in a parking structure until about five in the morning. Misery! In these moments of foolishness, I would attempt to mask and lessen my severe social anxiety by drinking a few alcoholic beverages, hoping that would allow me to socialize peacefully with others minus the intense social anxiety. It temporarily helped until I crossed the line from tipsy to intoxicated.

The second episode occurred on a concert camping trip in Buena Vista, Colorado. I kept telling myself, *Stay in control!* I didn't. As the night went on, I continued to consume beer and then ate quite a few alcohol-soaked cherries. I was hungry as I hadn't eaten much that day. As we left the campsite to head to the concert area, I was starting to lose control. I recall walking into the concert heavily intoxicated. I couldn't make out what others were saying. I made my way to the stage area, where I took a seat (can't even tell you if it was on a chair or on the ground) and I started blacking out. I remember security coming by and saying, "We need to get him out of here."

The next thing I knew, I awoke in a tent on a cot. An EMT was asking for my ID and phone. I vomited several times in the tent. The EMT wanted to take me to the hospital to spend the night, but I was able to talk security into taking me to my friends' campsite. Upon arrival via his ATV, I waved good-bye to him and made my way into a tent until he'd driven away. On my own again, free from security and EMTs, I exited the tent and somehow made it to my car parked a good mile or so away. I slept in my car that night and awoke the next morning feeling miserable, much as I had felt in

Minneapolis years earlier.

Sobered up somewhat after the night's sleep, I left the parking lot and headed back to my town. When I got home, I vomited again. I was upset with myself for not maintaining self-control. I had failed again and acted like a fool. I think about these two incidents of being blackout drunk almost daily. It's embarrassing and I pray readers will learn from my mistakes.

The Minneapolis and Buena Vista examples of blackout drunkenness are examples of sin: drunkenness and foolishness that lead to regret. I've made very poor choices and thank God for His grace—without that, I doubt I would still be alive.

Exercise greatly helps my mind. As I park in the parking structure at the athletic club, I park in an area marked with the letters T–W. Here's what I have come to see those letters representing:

> T: The Lord
>
> U: Unity with the Holy Spirit
>
> V: Victory in Jesus
>
> W: Winning in the end (Jesus defeats Satan and makes him a footstool [Psalm 110:1]. Good overcomes evil.)

In addition to indulging in excessive alcohol consumption, I was a soda addict for many years. I mention this because soda, which is full of sugar and caffeine, increases anxiety and fuels depression. That's an important thing to note. I've opted to limit caffeine as well. It's nice to have a regular coffee now and then, but drinking lots of water and getting consistent exercise is paramount to decreasing anxiety and depression. I cannot stress enough the importance of exercise. It helps physically, mentally, emotionally, and socially.

Find something active you enjoy and do it consistently. I take walks and hikes and go to spin class. Assess your diet and activities, as these play a huge factor in how you feel, think, respond, and interact. Substance abuse and unhealthy eating and thinking are not the answers to life's challenges.

> **Life Lesson #30**: Answers are found in health and holiness of mind, body, and spirit, and these begin with a new mind-set: recognizing that we need a Savior, Jesus, and His empowering Spirit. We need to walk with God daily, hourly—by faith and with a steel determination to trust His promises and practice His principles, which include practical, healthy habits.

> Following Christ Jesus, we begin to produce the fruit of His Spirit: "love, joy, peace, forbearance, kindness, goodness, faithfulness, gentleness and self-control. Against such things there is no law" (Galatians 5:22–23).

If you need help for substance abuse or other mental health services, please see "Resources" at the end of this book.

9

Rogers Memorial Hospital

Because of my persisting anger, anxiety, depression, and OCD, I began to see a psychiatrist in 2003 at age twenty-nine. During that time I continued to enjoy sports, reading, and music but also still felt extraordinary stress and anxiety at work, with people, and over all my mental health issues.

I was having repetitive, senseless thoughts and behavior—violent behavior, constant worry, irritability, tension, and fear, including a fear of dying. I felt that life was not worth living. Among my worries was the fear of anxiety-induced sweating and that I'd lose control and do something regrettable. I was always keyed up and on edge. At the same time, I felt fatigued, had shortness of breath, and experienced chest and abdominal pain. I had trouble concentrating and making decisions. I was consumed by guilt, hopelessness, and negative thinking. I felt worthless and depressed and lived with thoughts of suicide. I was single, lonely, and plagued with social anxiety.

During my early thirties, I was working as a financial representative. I had a roommate, a college degree, and a good social support system, including my church. But still, mental illness kept me in a state of stress that seemed out of my control. One evening I had a handgun at my side on a lamp table as I watched TV. I was certain that was going to be my last day on earth, until my roommate walked in. His entrance was a blessing as my suicidal thought in that moment went away. I couldn't kill myself in front of someone. I believe I told my roommate "I'm just cleaning my gun." Little did he know I would often say to myself internally, "I'm going to blow my brains out."

In a medical manual I was reading, I highlighted my symptoms and found that I had high to moderate generalized anxiety, severe social anxiety, and OCD. The OCD had me constantly checking and rechecking things in many situations. I was a neatnik, so I was compelled to stay organized. My dream was to be totally paperless because I was constantly reorganizing paperwork.

The depression had started around age twenty. I felt sad, helpless, hopeless, worthless, anxious, and nervous. I had difficulty making decisions. I'd sweat a lot and worry constantly about losing control. Before seeing a psychiatrist at age twenty-nine, I had taken medication for five years. Still I had experienced no middle ground between nice and angry, but I was sleeping seven to eight hours a night and my appetite was normal. However, the social anxiety was unaffected by the med. I continued to experience daily panic attacks. Not pleasant. Despite my condition, I was surprised and pleased that I was keeping my level of function up as well as I was.

The psychiatrist assessed me as having major depression—recurrent and severe—with SAD (seasonal affective disorder) and severe anxiety, OCD (obsessive-compulsive disorder), and GAD (generalized anxiety disorder).

He often changed my medication to find the right balance and encouraged me to get into group therapy to help me better cope with the anxiety and depression. He worked with me to stop thinking in extremes—seeing circumstances as black or white—and to work on improving my interpersonal relationships and overall psychological condition.

I made virtually no improvement during counseling, and the medication changes weren't making a difference. I would often present a calm façade while experiencing boiling rage on the inside. Though I no longer acted on angry feelings, I was in constant fear of doing so and experienced a lot of "what if" thinking. I had difficulty making career decisions and dwelled on career options. I thought of getting a master's in political science or a degree in physical education. A military career was out of the picture because of my psychiatric illnesses and eye injury.

Since age twenty, I'd been on at least sixteen different medications. With some, I experienced temporary relief, but the fact was that I was dealing with longstanding, chronic emotional issues. If medication were the answer, I would have been healed more than twenty years before! I admit that because of pride, I didn't consistently stay on the medications.

Of all my issues, I came to realize that pride was at the core and that "God opposes the proud but shows favor to the humble" (James 4:6).

In 2004, I shared my OCD symptoms with a psychiatrist who concurred that the symptoms sounded like OCD. He pointed me in the right direction for help. I applied for outpatient therapy at Rogers Memorial Hospital. The therapy, an approximately two-month commitment, was beneficial. The treatment cost me three thousand dollars out of pocket. I was grateful my insurance covered the rest.

If you are suffering from OCD, I highly recommend you seriously consider contacting an OCD specialist for therapy. It could change your life forever for the better. Please *do* something.

My issues of anger, anxiety, guilt, and shame were tied into my sinful nature, which I needed to address. During treatment I kept thinking, *What's wrong with me?*

I was a six-foot two-inch, two-hundred-fifty-pound angry man who didn't like or trust anyone. At the hospital I was standoffish with the staff (according to a male counselor), still carrying that chip on my shoulder. I had a long list of things to overcome. I mentally reviewed every conversation to ensure I'd given correct information and was not rude. I wrote and rewrote what I had printed on personal checks, schoolwork, and daily to-do lists. When I did not follow strict compulsions, I'd experience anxiety and stomach pain.

The treatment center was on a beautiful lake surrounded by nature, and the counselors were very caring and empathetic, giving me peace of mind. Looking back, I think perhaps I should have been in their inpatient program rather than outpatient. At the time, I owned a home in Greendale and had a dog to care for—my reasoning for choosing outpatient care even though I scored very high on their OCD severity level test for inpatient treatment.

Intake paperwork included the following. Sharing these personal medical records with you, the reader, is to reiterate that mental illness is real life and needs professional attention—and to assure you that you're not alone and that help is available.

Identifying Information and Chief Complaint: Mr. Gallagher is a thirty year old, single, currently unemployed male who was referred for more intensive treatment of his obsessive-compulsive disorder (OCD) that was diagnosed two years ago.

History of Present Illness: Mr. Gallagher reports having difficulties with OCD type symptoms beginning at least at the age of thirteen. . . . Mr. Gallagher reports that he will be engaged in obsessions or compulsions seven to eight hours out of the day. . . .

He scored a 29, which places him in the severe range. He also has difficulties while driving, including contemplating what would happen if someone were to swerve at him or if he were to swerve at someone else, checking the parking brake, checking that his seatbelt is on straight and secure and that his doors are locked. . . . He has had difficulties with anger for the last ten years. He has not assaulted anyone nor has he been in any legal trouble, though he has punched objects. He will also be quite aggressive in sports and has verbal confrontations. . . . He notes that he has daytime sedation despite sleeping at least nine to ten hours per night. He has had suicidal ideation, but none within the last month and believes that he would not act on any such thoughts. He has no current active intent or plan. . . .

Despite the use of medication, he continues to have fatigue during the day; despite the use of medication, he still has high levels of anxiety; and despite the other medication, he still reports significant obsessive-compulsive disorder symptoms as well as difficulties again with anxiety and depression.

Diagnoses: (1) Obsessive-compulsive disorder. (2) Depressive disorder. (3) Frequent headaches. (4) Right upper abdominal pain of unknown etiology.

Recommendation Plan: Given Mr. Gallagher's level of symptoms, he has been admitted to the Partial Hospital OCD Program for more intensive treatment of his obsessive-compulsive disorder. Treatment will include cognitive behavioral therapy as well as psychopharmacology.

Community/Group Involvement: *Mentoring Program in Metro Milwaukee, softball teams, High School varsity football statistician. . . .*

Personal Information: What do you like the least about yourself? *Perfection and procrastinating.*

What would you like to change? *A lot. Improve confidence, better communication skills, be more open with others, lose weight, find happiness.*

With regards to your emotional health, what do you wish to see yourself accomplish? *Overcome/defeat/ manage OCD and no longer have to take medication.*

• • •

Sidebar: Regarding dating, I still fear women and rejection. I feel nervous around attractive women, and commitment puts me at great unease.

I didn't date much in high school or college, or even well into my adult life. *What if one of us gets hurt? What if things don't work out? What if we break up? What if we get married and then file for divorce?*

To avoid rejection, I'd simply not ask women out. Not asking meant no chance of rejection, no chance of anyone getting hurt. Problem avoided.

I was paranoid when dating. I met a woman online who lived in Chicago and we agreed to meet in Gurnee, Illinois, for lunch. I didn't bother shaving. We parted ways after lunch and later she emailed me and asked, "Could you not have at least shaved for a date?"

I responded rudely—my way of saying, "Don't try to control me." I realized I couldn't date because I couldn't *love* yet with the humble and whole love of Jesus. How could I love someone else when I disliked myself, a unique creation of God, purposed to love?

I lacked confidence. *Am I good looking enough to date? Am I funny enough?* Again, I was obsessed with mind reading and failed miserably at that. I cared too much what others might be thinking.

As I've shared with you previously, I came up with a way to avoid the heartache of rejection: simply don't date. Sure, I'd had some girlfriends in the past, but I was quick to find flaws with them because I feared commitment.

> **Life Lesson #31:** Not all of us are marriage material, but each of us can be used by God to lead others to Jesus—the most important purpose in life.

It would be a blessing to find *the* woman one day—an attractive and athletic believer in Jesus—but I'm determined that the timing and individual will be on God's terms, not mine. In the meantime, I'm working on becoming more transformed to be ready for all God has for me.

• • •

The initial evaluation at Rogers Memorial Hospital also included the following notations by a physician.

Contamination obsessions: concerned with dirt and germs.

Comments: ritual is to turn the key in the door, say "yes it is locked," count to five, re-check, then okay; patient counts to five when putting windows up in the car; between cleaning and organizing, patient spends several hours daily on rituals.

On the "Partial Program Anxiety Disorders Screening Tools," I answered yes to each of the following and indicated that my anxiety disrupted my work, social life, and home responsibilities.

1. Have you, on more than one occasion, had spells or attacks when you were suddenly anxious, frightened, uncomfortable, uneasy, even in situations where most people would not feel that way? *(Patient triggers: worries a lot, orderliness, not working.)*
2. At any time in the past, did any of these spells or attacks come on unexpectedly or occur in an unpredictable or unprovoked manner?
3. Have you ever had one such attack followed by a month or more of persistent fear of having another attack, or worries about the consequences of the attack? *(Patient says social anxiety is much worse in large groups.)*
4. In the past month, were you fearful or embarrassed of being watched, being the focus of attention, or fearful of being humiliated? This includes things like speaking in public, eating in public with others, writing while someone watches or being in social situations? *(Patient fears being degraded.)*

5. Is this fear excessive or unreasonable? Do you fear these situations so much that you avoid them or suffer through them? *(Patient anticipates the worst thing.)*
6. Have you worried excessively or been anxious about two or more things over the past six months? More than most others would? Are these worries present most days?
7. Do you find it difficult to control the worries or do they interfere with your ability to focus on what you are doing?

On the OCD checklist, I stated that while driving I thought, *What if this car swerved at me or if I swerved at them? Is the emergency brake all the way down? Is my seatbelt on straight and secure? Are the doors locked?*

Patient participation in program: four days/week (for Anxiety & OCD)

• • •

Notes from the first day of class: "Life is difficult. . . . Once you understand this truth, life is no longer difficult."[8] "Courage doesn't always roar. Sometimes courage is the little voice at the end of the day that says I'll try again tomorrow."[9]

There were assigned exercises with anxiety ratings.

Exercises with an Anxiety Rating of 1:

1. Put a cup/dishes in the dishwasher without rinsing it out with cold water first.

---

8 M. Scott Peck, M.D., *The Road Less Traveled* (New York: Touchstone, 1998).

9 Mary Anne Radmacher, *Courage Doesn't Always Roar* (London UK: Mango Media, 2009).

2. Watch the behavior therapist hang a towel without shaking it out first.
3. Mess up clothes closet for one hour and keep the closet door closed for twelve hours.
4. Put white and black T-shirts in miscellaneous drawers and/or separate by color.
5. Wash underarms without counting.
6. Brush teeth without counting.
7. Let roommates clean the bathroom.
8. Look at roommate's bedroom.
9. Throw newspapers in the recycling bin the wrong way.
10. Take cleaning supplies out of order.
11. Let roommates wipe off the counter.
12. Let roommates unload the dishwasher.
13. Put items on different shelves in the fridge.
14. Leave the car unlocked during the day in the driveway.

At the time of the initial exercises I wrote,

I feel confident and comfortable with moving on because I think these exposures have been overcome. The remaining exposures to conquer are putting black and white T-shirts in miscellaneous drawers, dissembling items from multiples of five to three, and to stop using a tote in my bathroom.

Looking at my exercises, folding T-shirts without the emblem showing will be difficult. Messing up my hats and shoes will be tough and will cause anxiety.

Things I still want to accomplish this week include calling for a donation pick-up, looking into skydiving clubs, looking into possibly getting another dog, calling to donate blood, seeing my dentist, and doing a final lawn cut for 2004.

Today, I had a verbal confrontation with my roommate. He approached me about me not passing on an important message. Apparently, he thought I listened to and saved his message. I may have saved the message but did not listen to it. I do not appreciate false accusations. It is his responsibility to check his messages, not mine.

The Milwaukee Bucks start the regular season soon. I would be content with a .500 season, especially with uncertainty at the point guard position. Go Bucks!

Exercises with an Anxiety Rating of 2:

1. Touch your dirty plate with your palm.
2. Touch the rim of your roommate's dirty plate.
3. Lay a towel in a pile on the sink without shaking it out.
4. Look at towels folded with the tag out.
5. Put a black dot on a white hanger and leave in the closet.
6. Look at a shirt hanging in the wrong direction.
7. Mess up the bedroom closet for twelve hours and leave the door open.
8. Discard an item from multiples of five and move to threes.
9. Mess up belts.

10. Stop using a tote in the bathroom.
11. Skip cleaning the bathroom once per month.
12. Clean only one half of the bathroom at a time.
13. Recycle mail envelopes without removing the sticky stuff.
14. Recycle an envelope with a picture window.
15. Park the car without checking the trunk to make sure it is secure.
16. Use the stove and go to bed without checking to make sure it is turned off.
17. Leave a lamp on while gone for the day.

Exercises with an Anxiety Rating of 3:

1. Put roommate's plate in dishwasher without first rinsing it off.
2. Look at the toilet with the seat up (at home or in public).
3. Think of leaving the car unlocked overnight.
4. Watch a therapist hang a towel without shaking it out.
5. Watch the therapist shake out the towel while I hang it up.
6. The therapist folds a towel. I take it home and put it away.
7. Put the towels in the closet in random order.
8. Fold T-shirts without the emblem showing.
9. Clean one half of underwear drawer only.
10. Look at roommate's closet without organizing it.
11. Spread cleaning supplies throughout the home.

12. Dust one object in a room only.
13. For twenty-four hours, leave the bedroom closet messed up and the door open.
14. For one week, leave the bedroom closet messed up and the door open.
15. Pair up one half of shoes.
16. Look at suits out of alphabetical order.
17. Mess up baseball caps.
18. Skip applying deodorant or three swipes if used.
19. Shave without repeating.
20. Look at roommate's bedroom area without straightening things out.
21. Recycle a laundry detergent bottle and rinse out with one cup of water only.
22. Recycle a dented can without tapping it.
23. Put cups away without them being flush.
24. Leave warmer on hot without a lid.
25. Walk past the dryer without checking for lint.
26. Do a load of laundry without cleaning out the lint first.

Exercises with an Anxiety Rating of 4:

1. Put your plate in the dishwasher without first rinsing it off.
2. Touch home bathroom faucet.
3. In public, leave a crumpled paper towel on the sink.
4. Put a paper towel in an overflowing garbage can.
5. Take one sweatshirt out of a pile of five.

6. Give away a dress shirt.
7. Put a wrong item in the bathroom tote.
8. Discard mail with the sticky substance left on it or without shredding it.
9. Only wipe the kitchen counter once per day.
10. Leave the car window open a hair.
11. Turn stove on and off and leave home without checking it.
12. Lightly cross off an item from daily schedule.
13. Do not file a financial statement in binder.
14. Sign your name while the therapist watches.
15. Consult daily schedule only once per day.
16. Write one word in daily calendar and draw a single line through it.

Exercises with an Anxiety Rating of 5:

1. Touch my roommate's dirty plate with my palm.
2. Put a cup in the dishwasher without rinsing it off first.
3. Urinate at home without wiping off the toilet rim.
4. Touch a public bathroom faucet.
5. Touch home flusher.
6. Leave toilet seat up at home.
7. Touch dust.
8. Place a sweatshirt on a sweater stack.
9. Put a white T-shirt in the black T-shirt drawer.
10. Mess up ties.

11. Screw in a lightbulb without counting.
12. Walk by a light switch without checking.
13. Move knickknacks slightly.
14. Leave blinds at different heights overnight.
15. Buy and use a generic tote and get rid of an older Rubbermaid tote.
16. Leave shower curtain one half closed.
17. Look at dust (without blowing it away).
18. Discard junk mail without opening it.
19. Discard a stack of mail for trash without checking.
20. Take CDs/DVDs/books out of order.
21. Write one word messily.
22. Hand-label a file.
23. Do not cross off one week's worth of activities in daily calendar.

Exercises with an Anxiety Rating of 6:

1. Put roommate's plate in the dishwasher without rinsing it off.
2. Put silverware in the dishwasher without rinsing it off.
3. Urinate in public restroom without wiping off the rim of the toilet.
4. Touch public toilet flusher.
5. Touch home toilet seat.
6. Leave the toilet seat up in public.
7. Use home or public toilet, splash water on the sink and do not wipe it up.

8. Leave a drawer and cabinet door open.
9. Touch dirt and do not wipe off hand.
10. Do grooming routine out of order.
11. Recycle a laundry detergent bottle without rinsing it out.
12. Look at a cup ring on the counter and do not wipe it up.
13. Hang a towel in public and at home without shaking it out.
14. At home, put garbage in an overflowing can.
15. Fold a towel without shaking it out and then shake a towel and fold wrong.
16. Fold a towel with the tag out and leave it like that in a cabinet.
17. Use different colored hangers.
18. Leave a shirt in the closet hanging in the wrong direction.
19. Mess up shirts by brand/season/type.
20. Completely mess up knickknacks.
21. While in the bathroom, let the blinds hang at different heights.
22. Make a different number of swipes while applying deodorant.
23. Do not recycle a laundry detergent bottle.
24. Discard an aluminum can without rinsing it out.
25. Leave crumbs on the kitchen counter.
26. Put cups away in the wrong order.
27. Lock the deadbolt without counting to five.

28. Do not cross off completed items on the daily calendar.
29. Do not write schedule in daily calendar for one day.
30. Write one word messily/slowly.
31. Write in datebook without rewriting.
32. Take bill binder out of alpha order.
33. Make a fake job note for old job.
34. Write a paragraph with a grammar error.
35. Misspell a written word.
36. Take a multiple choice test without reviewing it.
37. Write a personal check without rewriting it at home.
38. Do not make a daily list for one day.
39. Leave a lamp on overnight.
40. Leave a light switch half off.

Exercises with an Anxiety Rating of 7:

1. Put roommate's dishes in the dishwasher without rinsing it off first.
2. Hold roommate's silverware without running through water.
3. Sit on a public toilet without inspecting the seat.
4. Touch a public toilet seat.
5. Put lint on a towel and hang it up.
6. Fold a towel the wrong way without shaking it out.
7. Intermix all T-shirts.
8. Leave the blinds at different heights while at work.
9. Leave the soap and shampoo out of order.

10. Do not spray down the shower after use.
11. Recycle an aluminum can with a small amount of soda in it.
12. Throw away a newspaper or a magazine.
13. Dust off half a table only.
14. Mess up the food cabinet.
15. Put silverware away wrong.
16. Mix winter and summer clothing items in the garage.
17. Park the car without checking it.
18. Leave the car unlocked in the driveway overnight.
19. Mess up the bill binder.
20. Write a paragraph without reviewing it.
21. Write a personal check in public without rewriting.

Social Anxiety Scale (11-17-2004). The following activities cause anxiety.

1. Telephoning in public.
2. Participating in small groups.
3. Eating in public places.
4. Drinking with others in public places.
5. Talking to people in authority.
6. Acting, performing, or giving a talk in front of an audience.
7. Going to a party.
8. Working while being observed.
9. Writing while being observed.

10. Calling someone I don't know very well.
11. Talking with people I don't know very well/meeting strangers.
12. Urinating in a public bathroom.
13. Entering a room when others are already seated.
14. Being the center of attention.
15. Speaking up at a meeting.
16. Taking a written test.
17. Expressing appropriate disagreement or disapproval to people.
18. Looking people in eye that I don't know very well.
19. Giving a report to a group.
20. Trying to pick up someone of the opposite sex.
21. Returning goods to a store where returns are normally accepted.
22. Giving an average party.
23. Resisting a high pressure salesman.

Miscellaneous personal notes included . . .

Lakehouse #3, 2nd floor, trees, parking, residential, eating disorders, lights, Sawyer Road exit, 31 miles one way, 10/18-12/09/2004, basement, bedrooms, clock, blinds, leather seats, peaceful, quiet, isolated, stay responsible, so what?

Notes on the last day of class: fears

Core fears: I will get sick and die. People will think I am a slob and I won't have friends. If things are not perfect, then I am a failure. My identity will be

> stolen and I will then suffer financial ruin. My home will catch fire if the stove is not checked, and I would be responsible for my dog being unable to escape. People will think I am unreliable and not dependable. People will think I am stupid. I will hurt someone or be arrested or go to jail. I will end up alone and unable to maintain healthy relationships.

Other miscellaneous notes I took:

> One and done (my attempt to not recheck things), eye injury, OCD, dysfunction: anger, protection, fights, death, high school, authority, college, sports, confrontation, depression, medications, anxiety, procrastination, jobs, over-thinking, mumbling, stomach pain, strained relationships. Goals: be positive, trust yourself, do not count, breathe, coach baseball, write, politics, real estate, carpentry, a master's degree in political science.

The truth is, I was still angry on two accounts: First, the eye injury I suffered at age four while playing with sticks at our neighbor's home, which rendered me almost blind in my right eye, subjected me to a life of hurtful comments and rude statements about the thickness of my right eyeglass lens. I still held anger over all those comments. Second, I was still angry about my dysfunctional youth. The injury and my childhood led me into such anxiety, paranoia, sadness, and dark depression that I dwelled in survival mode instead of abundant life.

Now I know I have a choice. My anger was a rotting branch that needed to be pruned for my further transformation in Jesus (John 15:2). I'm a growth in progress like all trees that must be pruned to thrive—trees that will eventually offer shade and fruit for others. Here's a powerful metaphor:

> **Life Lesson #32**: "Willows are one of the most popular tree species in the United States. Highly resistant to diseases and temperature changes, they can thrive in many different climates. They are also one of the best species of privacy tree as their distinctive leaves create a lot of coverage for your property. They grow very quickly—up to six feet per year—and can live for up to 30 years. The willow tree, however, is also somewhat high-maintenance; their roots are famously aggressive in their search for water and can damage pipes and pavement if not properly controlled. Their fast growth also means they require more pruning than most other trees."[10]

While at Roger's Memorial Hospital, I participated in "Thought Challenging/Probability Overestimation." The process included listing my fears.

- I will get sick and die.
- People will think I am a slob and I won't have friends.
- People will think I am unreliable.
- I will hurt someone, get arrested and go to jail.
- I will never have a family of my own.
- My identity will be stolen and I will suffer financial ruin.
- My dog will die in a fire.
- People will think I am stupid.

---

10 "Which Trees Need the Most Pruning?" *Mr. Tree: http://www.mrtreeservices.com/blog/trees-need-pruning.*

- I will end up alone and unable to maintain healthy relationships.

The fears listed above were due, I strongly believe, to not obeying the Word of God.

> **Life Lesson #33**: Read God's Word regularly. Write and read your positive affirmations and gratitude list. Your mind *can* be trained to think truthfully and positively, which brings us to the first half of a key verse, 2 Corinthians 10:5: *"We demolish arguments* and *every pretension* that *sets itself up against the knowledge of God, and we take captive every thought* to *make* it *obedient* to *Christ."*

God partners with our willingness to take action. This verse doesn't say that God demolishes or that He takes captive; this verse is a call to us to take action with the empowering of His Spirit within us. To undo what has been done after forty-plus years of lies in my head was not easy; it took time and effort—and I'm still His work in progress, but I'm confident in the One who reigns in power within me. Do you need to do the same?

> Being confident of this, that he who began a good work in you will carry it on to completion until the day of Christ Jesus.
>
> —Philippians 1:6

Becoming "transformed" means that I must choose to take action and address my anger with the same *forgiveness* and *grace* that God, through Jesus, extends to me every moment of every day. I must remember that all of us face adversity in life that we each must deal with responsibly, remembering *we have a choice* how to deal with each adversity.

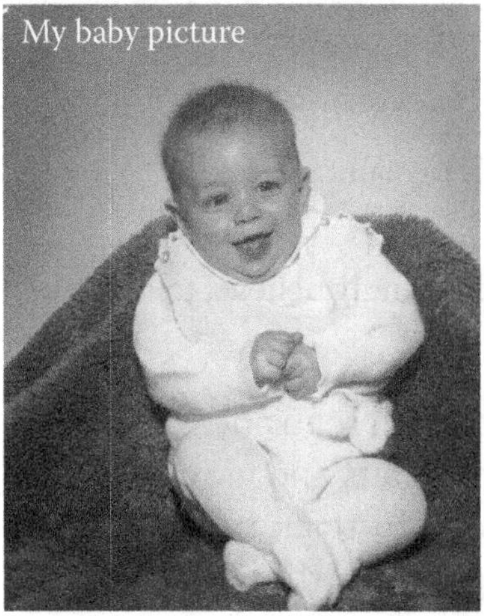

My baby picture

Look at those cheeks!

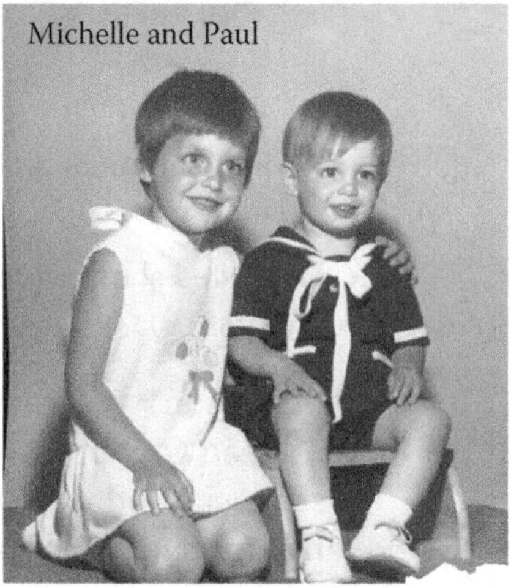

Michelle and Paul

She always had my back, even when I dressed as a Sailor!

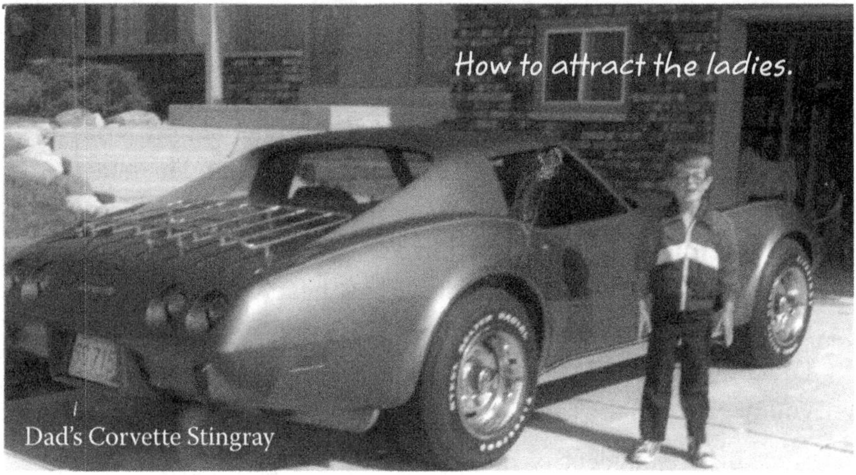

How to attract the ladies.

Dad's Corvette Stingray

I had no interest in fixing up this fixer-upper!

5151 South 60th Street

Rocking those tube socks!

Grandparent's home with siblings

Gotta love bell bottoms and Brewers baseball.

Little League Baseball

What a little stinker.

Bruno as a puppy

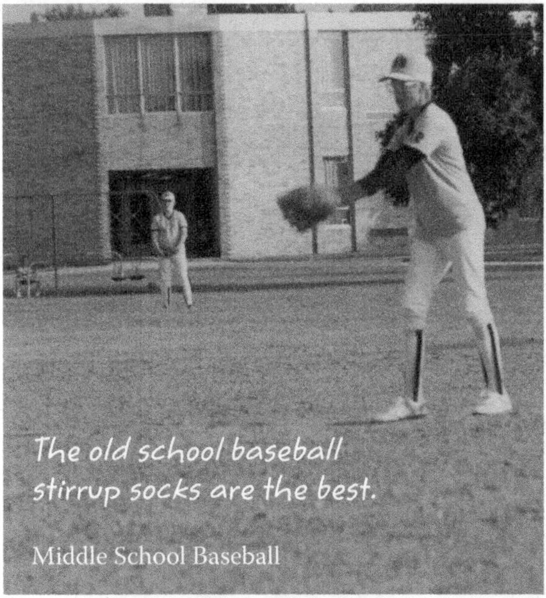

The old school baseball stirrup socks are the best.

Middle School Baseball

Rocking that sport coat and bowl cut.

8th Grade Graduation

Great kid!

Niece Kiley

Niece Lindsay

Motivated kid!

9030 Glenwood Dr

This is why men should have short hair!
Dancing with grandmother and mother. Love em.

Michelle's wedding 1996

You can see why my school classmates called me "chicken legs" and "daddy long legs" in middle school!

Family and Mother's parents

Dominating on the bump
by throwing strikes.

Panthers Varsity Baseball

Grabbing one of two rebounds
I averaged per game.
That's like one per half!

JV Basketball

High School Dance

Senior High School
Yearbook Photo

How did I trick the math teacher into giving me a passing grade to graduate?

High School Graduation

10

New Life Resources, Inc.

The next three years (2004–2006) continued to be difficult from both a mental health and employment perspective. Severe anxiety crippled me from holding a job for very long—most of them lasted a month or two and sometimes just for a few weeks or even days. Changing jobs so frequently led to more frustration and paranoia, which led to even more anger. My life was difficult—but what I didn't know in those early adult years was that God was molding me into the man He wanted me to become.

> You, Lord, are our Father. We are the clay, you are the potter; we are all the work of your hand. —Isaiah 64:8

After OCD treatment, I still experienced severe anxiety and bouts of depression. I was angry and frustrated over not finding or being prescribed a magic pill that would make my anxiety go away forever.

The medical bills for seeking professional help added up. I don't even want to know the total I spent over the years for counseling, medication, and treatment. I had spent easily tens of thousands when I could have simply found the answers for free in the Bible and at a biblically sound church. I'm not implying that counseling and treatment are not needed but rather that foremost, and at the root of all issues, is our need for Jesus, practicing God's principles, and trusting in His promises.

During the time I spent those tens of thousands of dollars toward my mental health, I bought a home in Greendale (2000). I lived there until 2008 when I lost my job (you're probably thinking, "Which one?") and my roommates. I shouldn't have bought a home in the first place, but part of the reason for doing so was to impress others—another example of pride and wanting others to see me in a certain way. How foolish. Purchasing a home was one of many poor financial choices I made. The home was too much work and I wanted things to be simple. They weren't. Still, God was using all my poor choices to further mold me into the man He'd created me to be.

> **Life Lesson #34:** It's at the juncture of true self-assessment and realizing God's love and sacrifice that we can move forward with no regrets, no looking back, *made free*. "So if the Son sets you free, you will be free indeed" (John 8:36).

> **Life Lesson #35:** Work hard, save money, pay off debt as soon as possible, and do not try to keep up with the Joneses (material things do not buy happiness). Tithe to a biblically sound church. Do what you enjoy (buy a gym membership or a

mountain bike, for example) and spend money within your budget on hobbies.

I came across a Christian counseling service in Waukesha—or rather God led me there. They were great. I think it's vital to find a true Christian counselor.

New Life Christian Counseling Resources

Initial Psychiatric Evaluation (counselor notes)

Chief concerns: OCD, anxiety, depression. OCD since age thirteen; treatment for depression at age twenty; recent breakup with a girlfriend; concern for safety, checking, symmetry, counting, collecting, shopping, hoarding, CDs/books, fear of failure, procrastinates, lack of confidence, unable to hold a job, difficulty making decisions, sorts papers and receipts, depression, sleeps a lot, hopeless, doesn't want to live. . . .

AODA history: alcohol use and a history of drunkenness.

Developmental stages: Neglect and teasing in school.

History of trauma: Emotional. . . .

Symptom review: Suicidality, guilt, withdrawal, poor self-esteem, anger/irritability (bad temper, problems with authority), verbal/physical aggression, OCD (excessive shopping). Client has stomach pain, feels uneasy in public, thinks others are talking about him, and thinks others perceive him negatively.

Impairment: Psychosocial and occupational.

• • •

Mental Status Exam (counselor notes)

Facial expression: Masked.

Mood: Depressed and anxious. . . .

Impressions: Long-standing mental health issues, debilitating OCD, his functioning is severely impaired, contributing factor to his difficulties is social anxiety, as an adult has had 20+ jobs and when he perceives a threat, he quits, his jobs are below his education and intellectual capacity, depression is long-standing and chronic, bad temper/poor frustration tolerance, and poor coping skills.

Treatment Plan: Presenting Problems: OCD, history of dysfunction, anger, relationship difficulties/fear of commitment, eye injury, impulsivity, poor attentional processing, anger/short fuse, occasional word-finding difficulties, somatic complaints, socially anxious, problems with authority, depression.

Goals: Resolve anger, grieve losses, resolve origin issues, address OCD, self-care.

• • •

Social History Questionnaire: 02/22/2006 (Paul's notes)

Expectations Regarding Therapy:

In a few words, what do you think therapy is all about? *Opening up, honesty, commitment.*

How long do you think therapy should last? *Until change is seen.*

How do you think a therapist should interact with his or her clients? *Be a good listener.*

What personal qualities do you think a therapist should possess? *Sincerity, caring.*

How will you and/or your therapist know that you got what you came for? *Discussion.*

Thoughts:

What kind of person are you? *Analytical, organized.*

Underline each of the following thoughts that apply to you: *I am worthless, I am crazy/deviant, there is nothing to look forward to, I can't do anything right.*

Circle each of the following words that you might use to describe yourself: *intelligent, sensitive, loyal, trustworthy, full of regrets, worthless, crazy, considerate, a deviant, confused, horrible thoughts, conflicted, concentration difficulties, attractive, can't make decisions, suicidal ideas, persevering, a good sense of humor.*

Please underline the following items that most accurately reflect your opinions: *I should be good at everything I do; When I do not know, I should pretend that I do; I should not disclose personal information; Other people are happier than I am; It is very important to please other people; If I ignore my problems, they will disappear.*

Underline and describe any of the following that apply to you: *unpleasant images, aggressive images (road rage, sports, drinking), and lonely images.*

Circle any that apply to you: I picture myself—*being hurt, hurting others, not coping, succeeding (at some point), failing, losing control, being trapped, being laughed at, being talked about.*

What pictures come into mind most often? *Northern Wisconsin, vacationing in a warm climate.*

Describe a very pleasant image, mental picture, or fantasy: *Sunshine, palm trees, ocean.*

Describe a very unpleasant image, mental picture, or fantasy: *Loneliness.*

Describe your image of a completely "safe place:" *Grandmother's home in Merrill, WI.*

How often do you have nightmares? *Often.*

Is there a theme? *Being shot, not graduating from college.*

What do you consider to be your most irrational thought or idea? *Driving into oncoming traffic.*

Describe any thoughts that occur over and over again? *Orderliness of things throughout my home.*

What do you like most about yourself? *Well-rounded.*

What do you dislike the most about yourself? *Procrastination and a lack of confidence.*

Have you ever believed that you might or did lose your mind? *Yes.*

If someone disagrees with you, do you generally argue, or give in? *Give in.*

Do you often believe that you are getting nowhere or that life has no purpose? *Yes.*

When did you last think about suicide? *February, 2006*

When did you last wish that someone else would die? *February, 2006*

If your present problems continue, what will your life be like in another five years? *Miserable.*

What would you have written on your tombstone? *I dub thee unforgiven.*

What might others have written on your tombstone? *One angry, grumpy man.*

What physical symptoms do you frequently have? *Headaches, stomach pain, lack of energy.*

When you feel badly, describe the feeling you most often have? *Hopeless and alone.*

How early in life do you remember such feelings? *Age fifteen.*

Describe the circumstances most often related to those feelings? *Others arguing.*

If given three wishes, how/what would you change? *20/20 vision, no anxiety or anger, a career.*

Behavior:

Circle any of the following behaviors that apply to you: *avoidance, procrastination, compulsions, withdrawal, nervousness, difficulty concentrating, outbursts of temper, cannot keep a job, aggressive behavior.*

Are there any specific behaviors, actions or habits you would like to change? *Yes, those listed above.*

What are some special talents or skills that you feel proud of? *Athletic, intelligent.*

What would you like to start doing? *Exercising intensely!*

What would you like to stop doing? *Being anxious and procrastinating.*

How is your free time spent? *Music, reading, movies, sports, dog.*

Please complete the following:

I am a person *who holds onto grudges.*

All my life *I wished for better vision.*

Ever since I was a child *I have enjoyed sports.*

It is hard for me to admit *that I am not such a tough guy.*

One of the things I can't forgive is *my dysfunctional youth.*

A good thing about having problems is *overcoming them (adversity).*

The bad thing about growing up is *responsibility.*

One of the ways I could help myself but don't is *intense exercise.*

Feelings:

Circle any of the following feelings that often apply to you: *angry, restless, anxious, envious, guilty, depressed, hopeless, jealous, unhappy, sad, regretful, panicky, annoyed, conflicted, lonely, fearful, helpless, tense.*

List your five main fears: *Death, being alone, not finding a career, death of grandmother, death of parents.*

What feelings would you like to experience more often? *Happiness, optimism, energy.*

What feelings would you like to experience less often? *Anger, anxiety, guilt, tension.*

What are some positive feelings you have experienced recently? *Hope.*

When are you most likely to lose control of your feelings? *Around people.*

Please complete the following:

If I told you what I am feeling now *I would say I am thinking too much.*

One of the things I feel proud of is *graduating from college.*

One of the things I feel guilty about is *not being closer to others.*

I am happiest when *it is sunny outside.*

One of the things that saddens me the most is *my grandfather's death.*

If I weren't afraid to be myself, *I might open up and socialize more.*

I get so angry when *I am asked questions.*

If I get angry with you *I will be mean and cut-throat (overdo it).*

Present hobbies, interests, leisure activities, you enjoy or find relaxing? *Sports.*

Describe any community, church, or recreational activities you are involved in: *Mentoring program, Big Brothers Big Sisters of Metro Milwaukee.*

Friendships:

Do you make friends easily? *No.* Do you keep them? *Yes.*

Were you ever bullied or severely teased? *Yes.*

Describe any relationship that gives you: Joy-*nieces;* Grief-*people.*

Rate how you generally feel in social situations: *Uncomfortable/very anxious.*

Generally, do you express your feelings, opinions, and wishes to others in an open, appropriate manner? *No.*

Did you date much during high school? *No.*

Do you have one or more friends with whom you feel comfortable sharing your most private thoughts and feelings? *Yes.*

Describe any concerns about past rejections or loss of relationship: *Hard to forgive.*

Are there any concerns about your relationships at work? *Yes. . . .*

Please complete the following:

One of the ways people hurt me is *by underestimating me.*

I could shock you by *my strength.*

A mother should *love and care for you.*

A father should *support and encourage you.*

A true friend should *respect and support you.*

How would you be described by your best friend? *Competitive.*

By someone who dislikes you? *An angry man.*

Please describe any history: *Drunkenness, addiction.*

What kinds of things make you angry? *Mean people and those that are arrogant.*

What do you do with your anger? *Bottle it up until I explode.*

Sequential History:

Please outline your most significant memories, experiences, and events in the following ages:

0–5: Eye injury

6–10: Sports

11–15: Dysfunctional youth/OCD

16–20: Death of grandfather/Depression

21–25: Social Anxiety

26–30: OCD

31–45: Depression/Social Anxiety/OCD

Over the course of time I was put on seven different medications, and a depression light lamp was suggested. It was then recommended that I complete a neuropsychological evaluation with staff.

Neuropsychological Evaluation

Paul is a thirty two year old male who self-referred for an evaluation due to concerns with inattention, lack of focus, and anxiety. He has a significant history of depression and OCD, and describes himself as socially anxious.

Behavioral Observations

Mr. Gallagher was pleasant and cooperative during all testing sessions. He developed an adequate working/social alliance with the examiners, which was characterized by an emphasized bravado exhibited mainly in the presence of the male examiner. Expression of affect was generally in the normal range with adequate variability, but occasionally abrupt with a serious demeanor. Concentration difficulties were noted during memory tasks when he was required to hold increasing bits of information. He often commented on his attention problems throughout testing. Occasional word-finding hesitancies were noted in varying degrees during tasks of verbal expression. Motivation was high for all tasks and he exhibited an achievement motivated attitude, which at times took on a competitive nature. No impulsivity was noted in his response style as he often re-checked his answers. He showed visible reaction to success and appeared aware of failures. Good frustration tolerance was noted. Movements were purposeful and goal-directed, with no overt confusional behaviors observed. Minimal signs of restlessness and fidgetiness were observed, mainly in foot tapping, leg bouncing and running his fingers through his hair. Speech was characterized by normal rate, volume and fluency. Initiation for conversation was good, and he responded well to humor. Thought processes were organized and coherent with no overt delusions or psychotic thinking observed. Problem solving was approached in a systematic and deliberate manner. Proper social inhibitions and social graces were adequately demonstrated.

Test Results

Mr. Gallagher's responses on the tests indicate a moderate level of depressive symptoms. He acknowledged self-disappointment, guilt, pessimism about the future, worthlessness, indecision, and a lack of energy. He experiences suicidal thoughts with no intention of self-harm. His responses are suggestive of moderate symptoms of anxiety. Severe symptoms of abdominal discomfort, an inability to relax, a fear of dying, and a fear of the worst happening were indicated with moderate fears of losing control. Mild symptoms of heart racing, feeling terrified, nervous, scared, unsteady, and shaky were also acknowledged.

Responses suggest clinically significant difficulties overall. Severe difficulties with activating and organizing himself to work, managing affective interference, sustaining energy and effort, and maintaining attention were endorsed. Mild difficulties were noted in the ability to utilize working memory and recall.

Results indicate that Mr. Gallagher responded in a self-deprecating manner with a subsequent tendency to magnify the presence of symptoms. With this in mind, he appears to be experiencing significant depressive symptoms and inner conflict. On the one hand, his downcast and depressive mood triggers a withdrawal from personal relationships. However, he dreads being alone or isolated from others. He tends to expect social disappointment and pain in relationships, leading to insecurity. This contributes to lowered self-esteem and a pessimistic view of life. He expects failure and anticipates/dreads humiliation. This appears to be grounded in a past history of being criticized or disapproved of. The vicious cycle here is that his irritability and sulky mood brings about the very social rejection or commentaries that he dreads. He appears aware of this process and becomes dissatisfied and angry with himself. It is difficult for Paul to experience freedom and to pursue pleasures without discontent and conflict, thus withdrawing from situations that might bring him relief from inner conflict. He has come to accept his painful state, believing that he possesses few positive attributes that he can rely on to find satisfaction with his life. Since he tends to not be aware of admirable qualities in himself, he may succumb to believing that his life is destined to be full of disappointment and discouragement. He may internally believe that he deserves victimization and suffering. In the end, his isolative behavior and anticipation of disappointment perpetuates a negative cycle of underlying anxiety inhibiting him from establishing fulfilling relationships. These dynamics appear to be a fairly stable component of his personality and are likely to influence his reactions across situations. He expects the worst and may actually undermine his own happiness or contentment.

Results indicate an estimation of general intellectual ability. Verbal comprehension abilities were found to be equal to perceptual organization abilities. There was a significant discrepancy between perceptual organization abilities and processing speed. His score indicates a significant weakness in the rate at which he can process visual information and utilize visual-motor abilities.

Note that Paul's working memory abilities were measured to be in the average range. Slight imitations were noted in his ability to sustain focused and direct attention over time with indications of inattention in his response style. Above average to superior abilities were indicated in regards to the new learning of non-verbal materials. Above average abilities were noted on improvement on amount learned with repetition, immediate memory after interfering activities, and delayed free recall. Visual memory for recall of newly learned complex visual material was in the average range for immediate recall and in the mildly impaired range for delayed free recall.

His performance on a task involving attention to detail, planning and problem-solving was in the low average range. His ability to conceptualize the nature and demands of a task was in the lower end average range, with a mild reduction in mental efficiency in his conceptualization of a problem. Verbal fluency, another measure of mental flexibility and efficiency, was in the average range. Speech was fluent and well-articulated. The pragmatics of social communication were intact with good eye contact, topic maintenance and turn-taking in conversation. Comprehension was intact for following of verbal and written instructions, as well as for social discourse. Conversational speech was characterized by occasional word-finding hesitancies with confrontational naming being intact.

Diagnostic Impression

Mr. Gallagher's presentation during testing reveals a man who tends to strive for making a good social impression in his demeanor and achievements, while covering an underlying insecurity. Results of testing indicate moderate levels of anxiety and depression with significant internal conflict stemming from a tendency to expect disappointment from others. This expectation may cause him to withdraw, but goes against his desire to be with others, as he dreads being alone. His drive to impress others and to be liked, along with the expectation of being disappointed in the end, perpetuates an ongoing cycle of anxiety about being accepted. While not experiencing specific features of OCD at this time, he continues to experience general fears and insecurities, thereby meeting formal diagnostic criteria for Generalized Anxiety Disorder (GAD). Additionally, his expectation of being discouraged and criticized contributes to low insight into his positive qualities. He may believe that he, in fact, deserves to suffer and to be victimized. This internalized view of self, which may derive from disappointing relationships in his youth, appears to have carried over into his adult life, causing difficulties with interacting with peers and authority figures in the workplace. Given these results, he currently meets

> diagnostic criteria for Depressed Mood, Chronic.
>
> Results of self-reported measures and cognitive testing indicate varying degrees of attention difficulties. He feels that he experiences significant problems maintaining attention, activating himself for work, managing effective interference, and sustaining effort. Results suggest that he has overall average cognitive abilities, with a weakness in processing speed, indicating difficulty with processing visual information and utilizing visual-motor abilities. Test results also suggest mild difficulty sustaining attention over time and mild impairment with delayed visual recall. It is likely that these areas of weakness represent the negative influence of emotional factors on cognitive abilities. While there is evidence of borderline attentional difficulties (ADHD), the primary difficulties with cognition appear related to emotional/psychological factors.

• • •

Several times, I hit rock bottom.

When it comes to counseling and taking medication, my advice is to talk with a medical professional and take medication as prescribed and needed. I also highly recommend meeting with a pastor or someone with grounded biblical beliefs and a biblical worldview. We can research secular books and websites for answers about self-help and self-improvement, but absolute truth about these is found only in the Bible!

Reflecting on my time in Christian therapy, I'm thankful for counseling. I also feel strongly that medication is not the *root* or complete answer. In fact, I am no longer on medication; it was not a long-term solution for me. For some, medication is necessary; however, we must understand there are many who are unnecessarily medicated and many who are overmedicated and under read—as in reading the Bible and practicing God's truths. Again, there are cases of mental health issues that medication favorably addresses. However, the root answer for mental and emotional health is found in the truths of Jesus, who came to this world to die on the cross for our sins and rose to "new life," representing the new life believers have in Him. "For to me, to live is Christ and to die is gain" (Philippians 1:21)—referring to the eternal hope we have in Jesus, that when God deems my time or your time on this earth is complete, we will live eternally with Jesus because our faith and hope are rooted in Him. "Believe in the Lord Jesus, and you will be saved" (Acts 16:31).

> **Life Lesson #36:** Be thankful for the life and mind you have while realizing we are all sinners in need of a Savior—Jesus. Combine reading the Bible with a healthy diet and intense exercise. We are physical, emotional, and spiritual beings, so don't put all your hope in secular counseling or medication. Like the food pyramid we've often seen, let's consider the value of the following lifestyle pyramid based on God's principles:

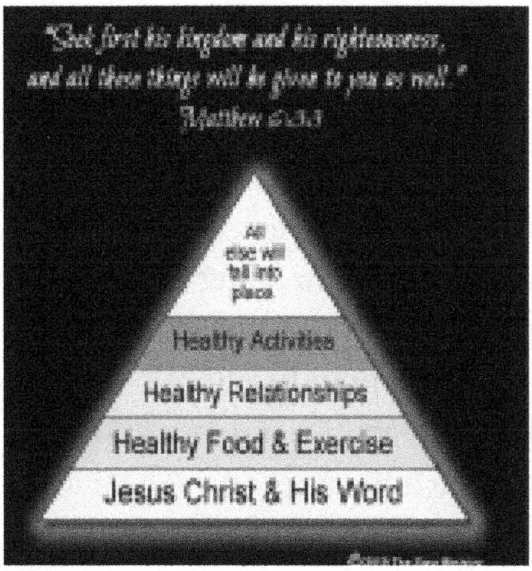

Jen Miller, *Now I Lay Me Down to Sleep: The Story of Sara. Used with permission*

11

Crossroads Counseling of the Rockies

When I was the varsity baseball head coach, I felt even more pressure to succeed, to win, to turn the high school baseball program around. A mountain of great expectations had landed on my shoulders, more so after I had been in the program for a couple of months. Taking a bus trip home from work on ECO Transit from Vail to Gypsum on a route that led past the school, I suddenly became overwhelmed by the weight of coaching the team. Panic rose in me. I thought I was going to vomit, and I felt absolutely certain, *I can't do this!*

One of my friends suggested I spend a week at Crossroads Counseling because it had been a life-changing experience for her. I thought that going through the one-week intensive retreat toward emotional "restoration and renewal" offered by Peter H. Kuiper would better enable me to make the transition between JV head coach and varsity head coach.

During my week under Mr. Kuiper, I took the following

notes, rooted in the belief that my identity is rooted solely in Jesus —not in myself, my job, or anything else earthly.

- Examine the heart! We have formal beliefs (saying) vs. functional beliefs (doing).
- Dysfunctional families are common.
- The enemy targets the heart with distorted thoughts, false beliefs, unhealthy emotions (inappropriate and unnecessary), and destructive behaviors.
- True beliefs are found in Jesus, who is the Way, the Truth, and the Life! From Him come accurate thoughts.
- The renewing of the mind takes place in the heart!
- Have healthy emotions and constructive behaviors.
- We cannot outwit Satan.
- The Holy Spirit is the Intercessor who convicts us of our sin, sheds light on the darkness, and leads us into *all* truth. "Lord, I pray you will open my heart to understand your truth."
- Information + Revelation = Transformation.
- I must have an attitude of gratitude!
- Discontent is a lack of gratitude.
- The OCD must be challenged and overcome.

Pain

In our pain, we turn to food, performance, alcohol, drugs, TV, exercise, avoidance, withdrawal, blame, complaints, work, self-pity, anger, shopping, intellect, pornography, sleep, co-dependency, spiritualizing, perfection, control, sarcasm, and various defenses.

- Smoke alarm example: Pain warns us that something is wrong!
- Pain identifies problems.
- Pain increases before it decreases.
- Pain is a gift!
- Pain is a battle for beliefs.
- What is your heart telling you?
- People turn to sexual sin because they feel cut off from love. This makes life only more and more complicated!
- Dandelion example: get to the root of the problem, not just the surface.
- I had defense mechanisms to survive childhood.
- Do the hard and the unfamiliar!
- I have wandered because of unbelief, rebellion, disobedience, pride, stubbornness, and a hardened heart. Return to me, Lord!
- In the valley of trouble is a door of hope (Jesus).
- Misery is the mother of change.
- Jesus is a Resurrection Specialist!
- Pain is not optional; use it for God's glory.
- Pain can be an effective teacher.

Failure

- Failure: embrace it, as it does *not* define me!
- We have a Savior!
- There is no condemnation for those in Jesus.
- Sanctified: growth, development, discovery.
- Two words: *temporary* versus *eternal.*
- The OCD must go! God is perfect; I am not. Say good-bye to and fire the OCD! Retire the OCD as it masks the pain.
- *Humble* yourself!
- "Lord, make my heart fertile ground for your truth to grow."
- I cannot fix or control others. I must love them and pray for them instead.
- "Please, Lord, bring healing to my heart!"
- I had feelings of not feeling valued, thus feeling rejected.
- I was seeking love and approval and instead felt rejection.
- J.O.Y. = Jesus, Others, Yourself (author unknown).
- Love yourself *as is*!

Expectations

- We are people-pleasers when we seek approval and love.
- Behaviors, performance, appearance, image, results, language—these are all external as we run on the "performance treadmill," and we cannot keep this up!

- Internal stress is when expectations exceed resources.
- Stress leaves one overwhelmed, anxious, angry, fearful (failure, rejection, abandonment, punishment, exposure), frustrated, resentful, bitter, depressed, hopeless, in despair, guilty, shameful (I am defective, lonely, isolated). We then go into "rebel" mode.
- A law-based system (external/achieving/compliance) versus God's grace (internal/receiving/surrender).
- Absolute truth and righteousness are given by God.
- Obedience to God means giving up control!
- The law says, "you have to," whereas grace says, "you choose to and get to."
- Let the Holy Spirit dwell within you.
- Whatever God expects of me, His promise is that He will empower, enable, and equip me to do it.
- When the lies of the enemy enter my mind—"Don't even go there!"
- External relationships: activities, common interests, performance, results, appearance.
- Internal relationships: based in and empowered by Jesus, one's freedom to be his or her real self, a choice-based love, a heart connection, and control from within.

Feelings

- Who I am is *not* up for vote!
- Is *their* problem *my* problem?
- Depression is anger turned inward.
- Indirect anger: sarcasm, passive-aggressiveness. Resentment and bitterness then settle in.
- Good news: God created us!
- I am afraid to let others see the real me.
- Relegated to the basement or apartment (feeling stuck). Come out of the dungeon!
- Be the real Paul! I am worth knowing and loving.
- Stop being relentlessly harsh on yourself!
- The OCD says, "You cannot fail; you are not allowed to fail."
- My sinful nature (lust, sexual immorality, drunkenness . . .) has caused many of my issues.
- I have been restored by the precious blood of Jesus!
- I am holy and blameless.
- I am learning, growing, developing.
- Yield to God's control!
- *Feelings* are driving my life. Don't base life on feelings but rather facts!

Identity

My identity is in my Heavenly Father!

- Greatest deception is when someone or something other than God is my source.
- Depending on others is the greatest hindrance to a healthy relationship. Become more and more dependent on God!
- I am emotionally thirsty: I need Jesus! He is a continuous supply of water and I will never thirst again.
- A crisis of trust: Do you *really* trust God? And are you willing to *submit*?

"Apart from me you can do nothing" (John 15:5).

- Do *not* fear mankind. Trust in God!
- His promises are true; therefore, stop living in self-absorption.
- Fire someone today—those living negatively in my head, rent free.
- Metaphor: Five rocks that represent my burdens:
    1. OCD
    2. fear
    3. paranoia
    4. anger
    5. depression

Sink these! Throw them all into the river!

- Who am I? Paul Michael Gallagher, a child of God.
- Why am I here? To love the Lord and others.
- Identity and purpose are vital.
- Shame is a private and strong emotion.
- Old nature vs. new nature:

    1. Sin nature: we project an image.
    2. External identity: I'd rather be a fake somebody than a real nobody.
    3. New nature: at the cross! An eternal seed.

World Identity

- World identity is earned rather than given; it is performance based, fluctuating, self-made, and self-centered.
- The world says, "You are what you did and what you do."

Christian Identity

- Salvation is a gift, a starting point of new life.
- Christianity is unity with God through Jesus, and it is constant. We are His workmanship. We have cause for celebrating who we are in Jesus; we were chosen by Him.

If this sounds like something that would be beneficial for you, visit www.crossroadscounseling.net.

12

Biblical Truth

In 2007, at age thirty-three, I was invited to The Ridge Community Church in New Berlin, Wisconsin (www.theridgecc.com) and started attending services. I liked my pastor and met good people. I took an interest in the Bible then. Where else could I turn? I knew alcohol wasn't the answer. I had zero interest in drugs, and I had learned material things are not the essence of true happiness and peace of mind. In fact, I often yearn to be a minimalist. Material things just accumulate, get in the way, and cause me anxiety. Whether you prefer less or more doesn't change *core* happiness and peace of mind. These can only be found in Jesus.

It was there, active in church, that I gave my life to Jesus and began the arduous journey toward transformation. For many, true change is an arduous journey—as it was for the apostle Paul (I highly recommend you read his transformation story in the book of Acts!).

> **Life Lesson #37:** Those who sincerely accept Jesus as Savior are not alone; we are empowered by the Spirit of God dwelling in us! As we focus on God's great love, renewing our minds with His truths, remembering Jesus's sacrifice that granted us forgiveness, and staying in tune with the work of the Holy Spirit in and through us, we begin to experience transformation.

It took time for me to realize that I must B.R.O.—Believe, Repent, Obey. This acronym was birthed in my thoughts while I was on a walk, reflecting about my sinful nature and recognizing it was time for me to "B.R.O. up!" The work of the Holy Spirit in me, with my decision to daily choose Jesus, has served to remove my desire for pornography and most of my sexual temptation since 2008. Praise the Lord! However, feeling inadequate and unworthy of a godly, beautiful wife, I still struggle with lust.

I grew up in the Catholic Church but wanted a contemporary message I could relate to from a biblical perspective. The Ridge, a nondenominational church, was what I had long been looking for.

I volunteered in Sunday school and later on the teardown team. But I experienced great anxiety even there—as with all other places. I was paranoid that I was being watched, mocked, judged, and criticized, just as I felt at work. At church, I also felt like a hypocrite because after a weekend of drinking and being sexually immoral, I'd show up for church on Sunday morning. The biblical *truth* is that we are all hypocrites at times because we are all sinners. The distinguishing difference is that those who believe in Jesus as their Savior are given grace and mercy to "continue to work out your salvation . . . for it is God who works in you to will and to act in order to fulfill his good purpose" (Philippians 2:12–13).

His good purpose is that we "act" from the new life we have in Jesus rather than continuing to act according to our sin nature, our human tendency. "If anyone is in Christ, the new creation has come: The old has gone, the new is here!" (2 Corinthians 5:17).

How?

> **Life Lesson #38**: We are to read and meditate on God's Word: "Your word is a lamp for my feet, a light on my path" (Psalm 119:105). We are to "take captive every thought to make it obedient to Christ" (2 Corinthians 10:5), and we are to "be transformed" to retrain the brain (Romans 12:2).

I had finally found a church that could help me work on turning my life around as I practiced my faith. It wasn't easy to do that, but my church definitely offered me the compass I needed.

Over time, choosing new life in Jesus, I've made positive changes to the point that I feel less hypocritical. Though we will not ever be sinless in this lifetime, we *can* follow Jesus as our lifestyle and mind-set and gain peace under His grace. I'm becoming more at peace under God's grace.

• • •

Colorado

In October 2011, I planned another move to Colorado to be with family. I needed their love, support, and encouragement. However, a week or so before the planned move, I found out that Bruno had lymphoma. I was devastated by this news.

Bruno had been my faithful companion since 2000—my first pet—and he was so full of life and love, often wagging his tail and kissing people. I found it amusing when people were afraid of him. He was an American Staffordshire terrier, also known as a pit bull. This breed gets a bad rap because of irresponsible owners. Bruno was the best dog ever, and I'm not biased. (Well, maybe a little.) If you ask those close to me, they would agree that Bruno was full of love and personality. People loved Bruno and Bruno loved people.

So, my plan to move to Colorado was put on hold. I wanted to take good care of Bruno and to give him every chance, which meant putting him through chemotherapy. (Having gone through this experience, I do not recommend chemotherapy for a dog, as it prolongs their pain and can greatly add to your debt. If your dog is in pain, putting him or her down is probably the best thing to do with a disease like cancer or lymphoma. Personal opinion.)

Bruno was initially given a good one to two years to live; his blood results came back as very healthy. I was told he was in better shape at age twelve than most dogs half his age! This news gave me hope that Bruno would make it to fourteen, which is a good long life for a dog. But that didn't happen.

December 4, 2011, was an extremely emotional day. That morning, my good friend Joy and her son, Jamie, came to say good-bye to Bruno. Although she wasn't a dog person, Bruno had grown on her when she and Jamie had cared for him for a week the previous year while I was in the Dominican Republic on a church mission trip. Now a year later, Joy was in tears as soon as she entered my home, knowing that Bruno didn't have many days left. We reminisced about him and all his love and silliness. I'm in tears as I write this. I really loved that dog!

> **Life Lesson #39**: If we can love our pets so deeply, just think how much deeper God's love is for us! In turn, we should love others. Jesus said, "My command is this: Love each other as I have loved you. Greater love has no one than this: to lay down one's life for one's friends" (John 15:12–13).

Joy and I shared Bruno stories for a while. It was a Sunday morning and I had no intention of attending church services; I was just too sad and emotional. But about 8:30, I showered and went with her and Jamie to church, where I could surround myself with other believers and good friends.

The message that day was powerful, and the worship was awesome. I cried throughout the service, thinking about Bruno and how great and loving God is. I thanked Him for all the fond memories of Bruno—the walks, the hugs, the kisses, his steadfast companionship. During a time of sadness and weakness, I thanked God for all my blessings. There was a time, early in my life, when I would have been more likely to curse God in hard times rather than tune my thoughts to the many blessings He's given me. Gratitude to God in the best and worst of times is part of the transforming work of the Holy Spirit for those whose faith is in Jesus.

> **Life Lesson #40**: We need to be thankful to God for all we have. Even in our darkness and thorns, whatever they may be, there is much to be thankful for.

I am thankful for family, friends, food, my health, clothing, car, and most important, eternal life. Though this life is often a struggle, I need to be thankful and remember that life on earth is temporary and God intends that I fulfill

His good purposes while I am here.

The three of us rode to church and back together, and, praise God, we had a great conversation about life, God, Bruno, and Joy's son. For years, I thought I was a worthless individual, but when my friend came to tears, thanking me for opening up about my past and in particular my anxiety, I cried. Joy said, "Because you opened up about your past, I'm able to see signs of anxiety in others. Thank you for opening my eyes to some things."

Years later, thinking of that moment still brings tears to my eyes. I felt Jesus using me to help others, and what a moment that was! This all took place in the car, with Bruno watching us through the window when we pulled into the driveway.

How awesome and powerful is the love of God that He would sacrifice His Son, Jesus, and raise Him to new life to demonstrate His love and power at work in those who believe in Him! I share this testimony of my life with you to glorify God and to help others through their adversities. It may have taken close to forty years of going through mental anguish to reach this time in my life, but forty years on earth pales in comparison to eternity and what awaits us there.

Cancer was taking its toll on Bruno. One day when he was breathing heavily, I took him to the vet, who advised me to put him down as soon as possible as Bruno appeared to be in pain and wasn't responding to treatment as we had hoped. What a very emotional day for me; I dreaded the day Bruno would die, and it would be all the harder if I had to make the decision to put him down. I cried a lot. I'd had so many good times and made such fond memories with Bruno.

During that difficult and emotional time, I gave my employer two weeks' notice because of my pending move to

Colorado to be with family. Bruno and I left Wisconsin for Colorado on December 19, 2011, and spent a night in a motel in Nebraska. When we arrived in Colorado on December 20, with Bruno breathing heavily and vomiting, I knew his time would be soon. I knew it had to be just days before I would have to put him down.

The vet we saw in Colorado recommended that Bruno be put down right away as his gums were discolored, his lymph nodes were enlarged, and his underbelly was red and obviously sore. It was time for my little buddy to move on. I was so grieved that I dry-heaved twice in the room where Bruno took his last breath.

If you haven't had a dog, this might be difficult for you to relate to. I can tell you that such a loss is emotional. I thank God for the support I had with me. We all hugged and kissed Bruno good-bye and cried. It was truly heartbreaking to see my little buddy injected with a needle that would send a chemical into his little body to shut down his heart and vitals. I held his paw until his last breath, and I kissed him good-bye. I loved him so much.

> *Parents*: Please love your kids even more than I loved Bruno!

13

Finding My Voice while Losing My Mind

So there I was in beautiful Colorado, finding my voice (writing this book) while still losing my mind. I had talked about writing this book for a good eight years by that time. (Remember I admitted to procrastinating?)

I wanted to find my voice while I felt like I was losing my mind. I wrote while listening to Christian music. I recommend the following radio stations where you can also sign up for their "Encouraging Word" and "Verse of the Day": K-Love (www.klove.com) and Air1 (www.air1.com). Tuning into Christian music is a positive change I've made along with many others: serving in church, praying, reading my Bible, exercising, eating healthy, limiting alcohol and caffeine, and so on. These changes didn't happen overnight, as you know from reading my story. They've come with commitment and perseverance over time and have helped me tremendously to discover my voice and God's, to renew my mind and faith, and to gain a better understanding of who God created me to be.

> **Life Lesson #41**: All the little changes we choose to make day after day add up to a much healthier and whole life. Jesus said, "I have come that they may have life, and have it to the full" (John 10:10). That's His great love and grace to us.

Writing about my move from Wisconsin to Colorado started me thinking about the climate. Having been diagnosed with SAD (seasonal affective disorder), I moved to Colorado partly because of the weather. The weather in Milwaukee can often be gloomy and depressing in winter whereas Colorado averages 300-plus days of sunshine per year. One psychiatrist said my mind would benefit greatly from a warm-weather climate. I just may move to Arizona one day!

To help me regain my mind—by overcoming severe social anxiety—I'd often force myself to face social situations like playing softball and kickball because I also greatly feared becoming a hermit. It was my tendency to want to stay home and watch sports on TV. Instead, I'd force myself to play sports and socialize. Though these activities made me extremely uncomfortable, I knew I was choosing a path toward better emotional, mental, and physical health that would pay off in the long run. Panic attacks are normal in my life, but that doesn't mean I have to live in fear and be ruled by those attacks.

> **Life Lesson #42**: Pray through the dark times while focusing on breathing: inhale deeply and slowly through your nose and exhale slowly through your mouth. Be present in the moment with your Creator.

> **Life Lesson #43:** Talk with someone who is supportive and trusting. If you don't have such a person in your life, become active with a biblically sound church, investing time serving others. I also encourage you to find a Christian counselor who specializes in your particular area of need.

Believers in Jesus who are also mentally and emotionally healthy are best equipped to help you manage your anxiety and other mental health concerns and see you through the dark times. I feel strongly about surrounding oneself with Christ followers because they have faith and hope in the power of God and His empowering Holy Spirit that unbelievers do not have. In 1 Corinthians 12, the apostle Paul spoke to the body of Jesus (the church), about the Holy Spirit and the gifts He imparts that encourage us through life:

> About the gifts of the Spirit, brothers and sisters, I do not want you to be uninformed. . . . There are different kinds of gifts, but the same Spirit distributes them. . . . to each one the manifestation of the Spirit is given **for the common good**. . . . All these are the work of one and the same Spirit. . . . For we were all baptized by one Spirit so as to form one body—whether Jews or Gentiles, slave or free—and we were all given the one Spirit to drink. . . . Now you are the body of Christ, and each one of you is a part of it. . . . I will show you the most excellent way.
>
> —1 Corinthians 12:1, 3, 7, 11, 13, 27, 31; emphasis mine

Relationships with Christ followers are priceless and powerful. We were created for relationship with others and with God through Jesus. My sister, Michelle, is truly a blessing in my life. I seriously wonder if I would even be here today had I not opened up to her about my mental illness.

> **Life Lesson #44:** Open up to someone as a starting place—a sibling, parent, friend, school counselor, coach, psychologist, pastor. There *are* trusted people who will listen and help. Find them and let them in.

> **Life Lesson #45:** Learn about anxiety and other mental health issues—not only for your own benefit but to be a help to others. There are many helpful websites and books, and foremost, the Word of God is ripe with wisdom about health.

> **Life Lesson #46:** Keep a daily routine and take life one day at a time, one moment at a time, one breath at a time. If *I* can do this, *you* can too.

I'm a big note taker, one of my daily routines that has become a *healthy* habit rather than so much an OCD habit. Some things I document are rather silly but doing so helps me remember what needs to be done and stay on track and focused. Making notes helps my daily routine to be consistent, and consistency is important and healthy.

When I moved to Colorado, I wanted to start doing things I had long put off. These included blogging, writing this book, and coaching baseball. (Check marked! I accomplished all three.)

I learned a lot about life while coaching the great game of baseball. It all started in 2012 when I began serving as a Little League assistant coach, a position I held through 2014.

On March 16, 2015, I held my first baseball practice as a Little League Juniors head coach in Colorado. I cashed in a $10,000 retirement fund so I could focus on coaching and writing (this book) for three months.

I went to the first gathering, where we had team introductions, covered season expectations (safety, respect, sportsmanship, fundamentals, fun, winning), and then held a practice. The boys, ages thirteen to fourteen, didn't know I was having a panic attack! Though I had played baseball in high school, I'd had no coaching experience. I'd had some anxiety as an assistant coach for three years, but when I took over as head coach, the severe anxiety and high expectations set in.

While driving home, I spoke on the phone with Michelle and lost it, crying. She was fearful that I was suicidal and insisted I drive to her home to talk. As I headed toward her home, I started to dry heave and have suicidal thoughts. *How much more can I take?* I arrived at her home while a pastor she had called was on his way to talk with me. I was a mess. The distress was a culmination of all the years of anxiety, depression, and fear of failure. I didn't want to lose as a coach.

Days later, I emailed my pastor and shared how I struggled with pride, procrastination, and perfection. I was honest that I was worn out from life and wanted to end it. I shared that I needed counseling and thanked him for being there for me. These steps were some of the healthy tools I gained in my journey through life. We need one another—solid Christ followers who will be there for us in our time of need, and we for them.

Our team had a successful season in 2015 as the Padres. We won the league. But had I really enjoyed our accomplishments? No, I had not. My mind raced as I planned practices and game lineups, wondered if the kids were having fun, wondered if the parents trusted me to lead the team, wondered if I knew enough about the game . . . I was still a people pleaser. An assistant coach, Laurence "Larry" Owen Wolfe, who died of cancer in 2018, was a positive influence in my life. He often reminded me to enjoy the moment. I had a hard time doing this as a perfectionist competitor. My attitude wasn't healthy. As a piece of advice, I challenge you to enjoy the moment and remember it's *not* about you—it's about the young people! Remove your pride and ego. Be humble, love, and stay positive.

Our Little League teams experienced success, but I still regret not giving some kids enough playing time as head coach of the Padres. I made it about me and winning. Looking back, I'd rather have gone 10–10 instead of 16–4 in 2015. I'd rather have been fair with playing time and teaching valuable life lessons through baseball. This age group is when a lot of ballplayers stop showing an interest in the game because of a lack of playing time or having an unpleasant coach. I like to think we had fun and won, which we did, but I wish I had better managed games and playing time. Teach life lessons! Oh, and have *all* kids at this young age experience playing as a pitcher.

After my time coaching at the Little League level, I made the jump to coaching at the high school level (2016–2019).

Despite my tendency to overthink, I like to keep things simple when coaching. In baseball, keep it simple by throwing strikes, making the routine defensive play, and putting the ball in play offensively. Put pressure on the defense! As a head coach, I was very aggressive with stealing bases. It's fun, so why not do it? More important than playing the game as described above are the life lessons learned playing baseball:

being prompt, taking ownership, building relationships, practicing good listening skills, learning good sportsmanship and teamwork, being coachable, showing respect, loving one another, and remaining positive.

I could write several chapters on baseball alone, but here I'll just share what I experienced.

My first year as varsity head coach (2018), we went winless. Talk about humility! I came in thinking I was a good head coach but quickly learned that the varsity level is a totally different game. It didn't help matters that we lost three key starters right off the bat (pun intended) and then suffered two more setbacks by losing a potential starting first baseman and a potential starting outfielder. It was a season of adversity, to say the least, but you know what? The parents were thankful for the efforts of the coaching staff, and the ballplayers had fun while making progress on the baseball field. The future was looking bright despite zero wins!

Year two saw us improve to eleven wins. Being the competitor I am, I still look back at managerial decisions I made in 2019 and plays that could have been executed to see us get to twelve or thirteen wins. But that wasn't reality. Reality was that we won eleven games, not my goal of twelve—still quite the turnaround from a winless season.

To my surprise, my coaching contract wasn't renewed for 2020, but that's fine. I cared too much by making baseball my identity. In truth, my identity is in Jesus alone, not in the game of baseball or anything else I work at. I'm perfectly at peace moving on, though I was initially disappointed and somewhat bitter. It took me many months to get over this non-renewal as I had given my heart to the baseball program. I had a lot to learn but was willing to do so over time. Life goes on!

> *Coaches*: Respect authority, take it one day at a time, and delegate duties to ballplayers, assistant coaches, and parents. Don't think you have to go at it alone as I often did. Be selfless, keep things in perspective, and remember the most important aspect: the eternal value of it all, which means above all else love the kids! Again, enjoy the moment! If or when I get back into coaching, these will be my intentions, learning from past experience.

While at a Colorado Coaches Clinic, I became friends with Keith Wahl, author of *Well Coached*. Please check out his website at www.completegameministries.org/the-book.

If you are seeking to find your voice while losing your mind, I encourage you to join a support group. I realize this is easier said than done—especially if you suffer with social anxiety. You're not alone in your struggles! I highly recommend Celebrate Recovery, a national organization that offers weekly local meetings across the nation (www.celebraterecovery.com). I've also listed additional resources in the back of this book. Please be proactive about your health in every regard: mentally, emotionally, spiritually, physically, and relationally.

I encourage you to read God's *transforming truths* in the New Testament books of John, Romans, and Philippians.

Also, Psalm 139 is one of the most powerfully uplifting passages written by the psalmist David about God's love and intimacy, the same love and intimacy He has toward you and me. I encourage you to read it.

14 Spiritual Warfare

For years I gave in to the lies in my mind instead of focusing on the truth I knew in my heart. I knew the truth but believed the lies! It was frustrating. Spiritual warfare has been one of my struggles over the years. It's a struggle for every believer.

Please believe this truth: Satan and his demons do, in fact, exist and he is a stellar liar and deceiver. He is not some mythological creature; he is real and the ruler of this evil, fallen, sinful world until Jesus returns to strip him of his power. Satan has attacked me over and over throughout my years.

One evening during Bible study, I sat on the stairs outside the room. I had zero interest in participating because of my extreme social anxiety. I tried to calm down through prayer and focused breathing. My paranoia made me think the members of the group were picturing me going into a church service and opening up with a gun. That's an example of how Satan filled my mind with doubts, fears, and anger. He didn't want me to participate in *any* Bible study because he knows better than anyone that "the word of God is alive and active. Sharper than any double-edged sword, it penetrates even to dividing soul and spirit, joints and marrow; it judges the thoughts and attitudes of the heart" (Hebrews 4:12). That's why the apostle Peter warned us to "Stay alert! Watch out for your great enemy, the devil. He prowls around like a roaring lion, looking for someone to devour" (1 Peter 5:8).

I was on the verge of losing it mentally and told Michelle. I was so paranoid that I was being watched, mocked, ridiculed, and judged by others that I believed those lies and wanted to retaliate. I was angry at others for what I *thought* they were thinking against me. For example, while walking to my car and thinking others were watching and judging me, I wanted to make a crude gesture at them. My effort, however, was to say nothing, to avoid being noticed, and to keep from offending anyone. I lived in contradiction. When talking to others, I would often wonder, *What do they want to hear from me? Will they like me? What if I say something mean, rude, or foolish?* Thinking I was being watched and judged, I would often intentionally say or do something embarrassing, thinking that act would somehow divert their attention to what I had just said or done rather than what I *thought* they may have been thinking. The reasoning within mental illness is hard to explain because it's often not reasonable.

Satan had hold of my mind, and that included thoughts of suicide. I had thoughts of driving into oncoming traffic on highways, so I'm not surprised when evil happens in society. As I've shared earlier in this book, the tactics of Satan are "to kill and steal and destroy" (John 10:10). We allow ourselves to fall into his traps when we don't stay alert to "watch out" for him.

> Worry occurs when we fail to live out the Word of God.

Thankfully, I now have a relationship with the Lord and know that God is the One I need to follow, the One who is far greater than Satan and the One who will win in the end. We each must choose which team we'll be on. I want to be on the team I know is more powerful and is going to win in the end. Without God, who knows how much more damage I'd be capable of inflicting on myself and others? Such is the case for each of us. We must be alert.

> Life Lesson #47: Satan lurks, attacks, lies, and deceives. The best way to fight Him is with the armor of God, which includes "the sword of the Spirit, which is the word of God" (see Ephesians 6:10–18).

For so long I was focused on time, age, and death, but we have no control over these! Time ticks away, we get older, and death becomes imminent. Yet, while playing outfield during softball games, I'd picture myself dead and in the ground. I'd wonder, *How and when will I die? Will I be left for dead? Will I be buried alive? Will I go to heaven?* On nice sunny days, I'd wonder how many more of those days I'd have left before my death and think, *This could be my last nice day*. At fourteen, looking at my social studies teacher (who was exactly twice my age), I wondered, *Will I live that long? What will I do with my life? What will I be doing at that age?*

My defeatist attitude was part of the spiritual warfare: *It's too late and I'm too old to do what I want to achieve. I'll die one day anyway, so what's the point?* I told myself it was too late and I was too old to get a master's degree and a career in law enforcement and follow other interests. I would read and inquire about a particular profession—like teaching—to learn what would be required, but I'd derail myself with the lies. *Too late and too old.* I would consider starting a family and think, *Who gets married after their thirties?* For a long time I considered writing this book—and finally did it—but the point is this: my mind-set was out of alignment with God's. If I could put something off, I put it off. This mentality prevented me from pursuing my interests and improving my quality of life. And it quickly ruined many relationships with women and employers.

I had a fear of failure, relationships, and loss. As I've demonstrated, I was competitive in sports to the extent that I was rude to teammates, opposing players, and umpires. I've since apologized to those I've hurt but regret the way I lived.

Worry is another tool of the enemy. *Am I insane because of my anger and anxiety?* I'd also worry excessively about money. I reached the point that I was drowning mentally and financially and felt there was no escape from my anguish. But there was—I learned the importance of being financially responsible.

> If your financial circumstance seems dire or you just find it difficult to make ends meet, I urge you to enroll in a local Financial Peace University class—a national biblically based program with local classes that will guide you step by step into financial freedom and peace: www.financialpeace.com/product/financial-peace. Scroll to the bottom of that web page and enter your zip code to find a class near you. I've also included this resource in the back of this book.

Comparing ourselves with others and feeling jealousy occur when we don't know our true identity. I would often compare myself with others, especially with two particular high school classmates. I'd often wonder what they and others from high school were doing with their lives. *Are they happy in their careers? Have they started families? How much money do they have?* It was nonstop jealousy. To this day, I have the tendency to allow my thoughts to digress, to want to play basketball, racquetball, and softball against my former classmates to prove I can compete with them athletically. Much of this tendency comes from my youth when I had such strong feelings of inadequacy and worthlessness.

Here are more examples of spiritual warfare that plagued me. Perhaps these will help you identify the spiritual warfare in your life and guard against these traps and lies of the enemy. I'm letting you into the mind of a mentally ill individual. This shows the importance of memorizing Scripture:

- Uncertainty with others. *What do I say? What does one want to hear? Will they like me? Do they like me?* Feeling programmed to say certain things, to be negative and put up walls as I didn't want people to know the real me. Being on high alert in public.
- Uncertainty about myself. *Who am I? What do I stand for?*
- Uncertainty about career path. Military, government, finance, teaching . . . ?
- Making poor choices. Fights at school at age twelve, chewing tobacco, knife incident to my right thigh.

- Feeling underrated and holding grudges in high school sports. Senior year, four teammates and I quit varsity basketball. I said it was because of the coach, but in reality it came more from a lack of confidence and severe social anxiety.
- Confrontational. My teammates would ask me, "You going to get into any fights?" Sure enough, within minutes I'd find myself talking smack to other players. A man once said, "Hey, he's at it again." Part of me sought and desired confrontation while also trying to keep peace and be agreeable. Confrontation was my way of appearing tough.
- Living in the past and regretting my past. Playing with sticks; getting average grades in school; not playing in or succeeding at certain sports; intoxication that led repeatedly to other poor choices.
- Unable to live in the moment or enjoy life and fearing the future. Unable to comfortably relax and watch a movie, feeling I had to declutter or read instead. Often mentally busy and worrying.
- Feeling tremendous guilt over leaving my dog for any period of time (even one hour), especially while I was in spin class. *Is he okay? Does he have to go outside? Is he hungry? Did he have a seizure? Is he dead?*
- Focusing on my flaws and imperfections, second-guessing everything I said and did and everything others said and did—the coulda, woulda, shoulda mentality. *When is the last time I saw so-and-so? What did I say? Did I lie? Am I cool and funny? Are they mad at me? Am I liked and respected? What*

do people say about me? Am I being backstabbed? Who can I trust? Am I a bad person for having anger issues? Prior to job interviews, asking myself, *What will they ask? How will I respond? Will I mumble? Will I sound foolish?*

- Self-hating; defining myself in negative terms: fat, foolish, mumbling, blind in one eye, lazy, can't hold a job . . .
- Hard on myself to the point that doing anything was almost impossible; having impossibly high expectations for myself. "Even higher than God's," a counselor once told me.
- Dissatisfied after I'd done my best to complete a task. Paralyzed by what I thought were others' impossible expectations of me.
- Feeling worthless as a person and worthless in whatever I did. Feeling that I appeared arrogant to others when in fact I had minimal confidence and minimized my feelings.
- Feeling I was in the way. *I'm a nuisance to others.*
- Feeling undeserving of love and attention. *Am I wasting their time?*
- Feeling immature, childish, and not respected. *I'm a grown man physically but twelve years old emotionally.*
- Depressed and hopeless. Becoming severely depressed at 4:00 p.m. in Milwaukee.
- Self-defeating mentality. When golfing with coworkers, I'd yell at myself before taking my back swing. Coworkers would respond, "Don't be so negative and hard on yourself."

- Perfectionist mentality but lacking energy. I had exercise equipment at home but no desire to use it. Making excuses: *I have minimal energy; it isn't worth my time and effort. It won't do anything for me. There are things I need to organize and read.*
- Wanting what I did not have. A particular job, a certain home, a specific car, a woman.
- Experiencing panic attacks. I somehow managed to play softball for many years while having panic attacks. In the aftermath of 9/11, I felt claustrophobic and had panic attacks on the racquetball court each time I'd play. I had panic attacks and severe anxiety when introducing myself to others. The list of things that brought on panic attacks seems endless.
- Avoiding people at all costs and caring what total strangers might think of me. At high school football games I'd panic and think, *Oh no, there's so-and-so. What if they ask what I'm doing with my life? Should I make something up to appear successful?* I wouldn't greet people or say good-bye and I'd disappear from social events.
- Going to extremes not to be seen or heard; not wanting to be seen by others, heard about, or talked about. Wanting to live like a hermit. Thoughts of living in a remote cabin in Colorado with three dogs, no people.
- Apathy with a survive-the-day mentality in high school and at jobs. *One day death shall happen and hopefully soon.*
- Lacking organization; making excessive attempts and being obsessed with paperwork. Recycling

and shredding in an attempt to simplify things. The more I tried to get organized, the more unorganized I became.

- Obsessed with celebrities' ages. *How old is that athlete or actor?*
- Obsessed with sports; a fanatic, not wanting to miss a second. Planning my days around sports on TV.
- Obsessed with reading, researching, writing, and putting tremendous pressure on myself to stay up to date on current events. Pushing myself to know almost everything in the news; feeling obligated to read everything I could get my hands on; looking for new things to learn and needing to know everything as I wanted so badly for others to view me as smart.
- Obsessed and perfectionistic with accuracy and consistency. Things had to be a certain way. Feeling I had to buy certain products: running shoes, blue jeans, kitchen items, tools, storage items, camping gear. I had to buy postage stamps and drop off my mail at the same post office.
- Angry with myself when procrastinating. A road bike sat unused in my basement for ten years, so I sold it. I was advised to invest in a depression lamp but have yet to use it after purchasing it many years ago.
- Fear of relationships and loss.
- Fear of change and criticism.
- Fear of offending others in social settings, which might lead to fisticuffs. *What do others want me to do and say? Is what I say obvious? Am I Captain*

Obvious? If I say nothing I will not be noticed and not offend people.

- Fear of failure, disappointing others; unable to say no to others. Fearing that telemarketers might not like me or might cry if I say no. I specifically remember not being able to say no to a firefighter who called for fundraising, though I had very few funds at that time. I thought, *This man is depending on me to donate. If I don't, the fire station will close.*
- Fear of rejection. Fear of simply saying hi to someone for fear of rejection. Looking away immediately after waving a greeting to someone. Avoiding eye contact for fear of not being smiled at or waved at. Seeking acceptance but intensely fearful of rejection, especially by women and popular kids. I kept a rejection letter from a police department on my bedroom wall, perhaps to motivate me but more likely because I was bitter.
- Fear that someone would think I'm a stalker.
- Fear of choking in public tied into my fear of being watched and judged.
- Fear I would show any emotion, especially anger, but my body language caused others to believe I was angry. What's wrong with that man? Why is he so angry? Afraid to show happiness. *Is it okay to be happy?* I thought that to be happy was to be weak. Smiling showed weakness and was a form of mockery. Believed people expected me to be negative and would be shocked when I was positive, thinking, *That is so not like Paul to be positive!*

- Afraid to use big words as an auxiliary officer. Example, sesquicentennial. Panic!
- Afraid to ask questions for fear of interrupting others. *Am I being too loud and interrupting when I talk?*
- Afraid to speak my mind. *What if I am wrong? Will people then think I'm a fool?*
- Afraid to talk about others as the conversation might be a setup to frame me.
- Afraid what others were thinking when I donated blood. *This guy probably has HIV.*
- Afraid of my own physical power and anger, wanting to fight but being afraid of hurting someone.
- Afraid I'd snap from being on edge.
- Blaming others for my personal issues.
- Poor attitude and being anti-authority. *Don't tell me what to do! Why work when one day I'll die? I might as well enjoy life and just watch sports on TV.*
- Often guarded, sensitive, and defensive. At the grocery store, I wanted to scream, "Get out of my way!"
- Trust issues. *If I tell someone something, will they tell others? Don't talk, don't trust, don't feel.* Trembling hands, including at work in mandatory daily work meetings.
- Paranoid when driving. *Am I in the way or going too slow? Will I be honked at? Am I in trouble? Is someone calling the police on me?*

- Paranoid about doctors. Thinking doctors were greedy and unethical, just after my money.
- Paranoid about people in general. Thinking others were taking advantage of me. Assuming the worst would happen; assuming people are bad, mean, unfriendly. For a long time, I saw human beings as my enemies, believing men thought they were tougher or better than me and women thought I was weird or odd.
- Vicious cycles: no job, no health insurance, no money, no coverage for therapy and medication . . .
- Severe anxiety ordering fast-food at a drive-through. *Who inside is listening? Can they hear and understand me? Did I mumble? Are they laughing at me? Do they think I'm overweight and shouldn't be ordering fast food?*
- Mental anguish when shopping; I'd walk into a store with tremendous anxiety. *Who's watching me? Will I see anyone I know, and if so, what will I say? What did we talk about last time? Do the employees and other customers think I look suspicious? Am I sloppy? Is security watching me? Do they think I am stealing? What if I run into another cart? Will there be a confrontation?*

  If using coupons, fearing that others would think, *That guy is so cheap! Keep an eye on this obese white gentleman. He looks like trouble. I can foresee him stealing stuff.* Or say, "Watch the gentleman in the blue jeans, sweatshirt and baseball cap. He looks like bad news." "Copy. We're on him."

- Anxious about public restrooms, especially at sporting events. Incidents led to verbal exchanges: At an arena restroom a man said, "Who's in there? What's taking so long?" I came out of the stall and asked, "Does someone in here have an issue with me using the toilet?" No response. I then said loudly, "That's what I thought." In a baseball stadium restroom, while I was using the urinal, a man said, "Come on already!" I didn't say anything as I left, but I did shoulder some guys on the way out as if to say, "Don't bother me." I was looking for a confrontation.
- Disliked people but loved nature—the outdoors, wildlife, birds . . .
- Lying and exaggerating the truth to impress others. Trying to keep track of all the lies.
- Being okay at night but dreading mornings.
- Expecting others to finish my sentences because of my anxiety and therefore no desire to speak to anyone. *If I start a sentence, maybe someone will finish it.* Often in a hurry to speak so I could be done talking and thus no longer be the focal point of the conversation.
- Not easy to talk with others, joke, or laugh. Feeling that to show emotion is to show weakness. *Does everybody here like me? Yay! Got to be a tough guy and funny at all times.*
- Preparing conversations in case I happened to see someone I know—friends, coworkers, softball teammates . . .
- Rehashing conversations in my mind. *Did I tell X and Y the exact same thing? There can be no*

variation! It must be the same word-for-word dialogue.

- Dwelling on mistakes, bad decisions, and poor choices. *What if I hadn't played with sticks; what if I'd gotten better grades in high school?...*
- Believing that others think what I have to say is irrelevant, so offering no verbal opinions. *Do people care what I have to say? My opinion is wrong, irrelevant, unimportant, and a waste of time.* I'd text or email to avoid the anxiety of conversation. I even emailed prospective clients while working in sales, allowing me to avoid phone conversations and any rejection that would come with those.
- Feeling I was annoying, weird, nosy, and interruptive when talking.
- Poor listening skills and repeatedly asking, "What was that?" I have a poor attention span, to say the least.
- Fight-or-flight mentality. No middle ground; couldn't negotiate or meet in the middle.
- All or none mentality. Pushing to read a book in one sitting or it's not perfect. Difficulty in finishing what I've started.
- Risky behavior. Driving 100 mph after drinking several beers, not caring if I died. Riding a motorcycle at 140 mph for an adrenaline rush and not caring if I died.
- Taking things personally even when a situation didn't involve me. Self-incriminating mentality: *It's all my fault.*

- Restless leg syndrome; unable to sit still. *What else has to get done? What did I forget to do? Whom did I let down?*
- Constant thinking and over-thinking; unable to let my mind shut down or relax. *Who has time to relax when so much has to get done and there are things to organize and things to learn?*

There is no other way to view those examples—the traps in my mind—except as spiritual warfare. The enemy wanted me to stay focused on myself, my shortcomings, my circumstances, negativity, what others might be thinking, and material things. He really wanted me on his team, but I've become determined that's not going to happen. I've switched to the truth team, God's team. Living in lies is no way to live. The freeing truth is,

> I can do all this through him who gives me strength.
>
> –Philippians 4:13

I needed to renew my mind before I was six feet under. To help combat the lies, I finally got involved with coaching baseball. Although I was in my late thirties, it wasn't too late! I encourage you to stop believing the lies, stop being proud, stop procrastinating, and stop being a perfectionist. It's not too late to fulfill your God-given dreams and purposes. If I can do it, so can you.

15

The Paranoid, Prideful Man

As mentioned, eventually I learned that someone else was behind my negative thoughts: Satan, the liar and deceiver. I learned this truth the hard way. By sharing with you, I hope you'll be better equipped to war against him than I was. Satan and his demons lurk and attack—that's his sole mission. To avoid his snares and live the abundant lives God desires for us, we must commit to Jesus—the one true power over Satan—as our central focus. First, by repenting of our sinful ways and forgiving others as God has forgiven us and second, by daily putting on the armor of God (again, Ephesians 6:10–18).

As we run toward the cross, we run away from the enemy. My daily prayer is for a strong faith, peace of mind, a loving heart, and thankfulness for all I've been blessed with—including God's forgiveness of all my sins—and I pray others will forgive my sins against them. I pray daily that I will be obedient to God's Word, committed to Him, and produce the fruit of His Spirit.

> **Life Lesson #48:** Once you become familiar with God's Word, *obedience* is the key. "To obey is better than sacrifice" (1 Samuel 15:22). We can sacrificially do all sorts of good deeds, but if we're not being obedient to God's Word, those good deeds are as "filthy rags" (Isaiah 64:6), hypocrisy, and idolatry.

It's important from time to time to meditate on the many blessings we have and handwrite a list of all we are thankful for. "Every *good* and perfect *gift* is from above, coming down from the Father" (James 1:17). This list exercise will bring our thoughts back into alignment with God's grace and goodness, lest we become prideful and forgetful from whom our blessings come. Despite the condition of our hearts, our minds, and our world, God keeps on giving good gifts that we too often lose sight of.

Here are the top twenty-five on my list of what I'm thankful for:

1. God (my Creator)
2. Jesus (my Savior)
3. The Holy Spirit (my indwelling Guide)
4. family
5. friends
6. good health
7. a roof over my head
8. food
9. clothing
10. a car
11. a job

12. a good local church
13. vision (successful cataract and Lasik surgeries in 2014 and 2015)
14. ability to read
15. ability to write
16. money
17. sports
18. ability to walk
19. twelve quality years with my dog, Bruno
20. Merrill, Wisconsin, and fond memories of time spent with Grandma Lorraine (1916–2016)
21. my two best friends, Michelle and Heath
22. ability and opportunities to coach baseball
23. heat and warmth
24. physical life
25. eternal life

There's something about physically writing things down that more deeply impacts our memory. I urge you to handwrite your gratitude list, refer to it regularly, add to it, and most importantly, share your gratitude to God through prayer.

I was a paranoid and prideful man, as I demonstrated in previous chapters, including the many instances of road rage. I was punched in the face by a seventy-eight-year-old man when I was twenty-four. I had the right-of-way to proceed through the intersection and as I was doing so I heard a car honking. I ignored it. When the other driver honked again, I responded with a vulgar and immature gesture, which invited him to follow me into a parking lot.

I chuckled when I saw that the occupants were an elderly couple. The man approached my car and asked, "Why did you gesture at me?" I explained that he was in the wrong; I had stopped first and was the driver on the right, meaning if we had reached the stop sign at the same time, I legally had the right-of-way. He waved his fist at me and said, "I ought to give you one of these, you young punk!"

"Now sir, that's not necessary," I replied. That's when he punched me. I was stunned. I exited the car and asked incredulously, "Did you really just punch me?"

His wife chimed in, "Don't hurt him!" I assumed she was talking to me, but my friends and I like to joke that she was telling her husband not to hurt me. I threatened to press charges for assault. The police station was literally fifty yards away and he was okay walking with me into the station. His wife, however, held him back. I warned him that if he pulled that stunt in downtown Milwaukee, he'd likely get assaulted.

We had both made poor decisions that day.

> **Life Lesson #49**: Every choice, great and small, has a consequence.

Another road rage incident happened in Greenfield, Wisconsin. I came to a stoplight at a freeway exit that pretty quickly turned from green to yellow to red, and I panicked. I stepped on the gas to get through the light. At the next intersection, a man pulled up next to me, rolled down his window and asked, "Do you always blow through red lights?"

"Sometimes," I said. He was upset and yelled something to which I responded, "Are you a police officer? If so, pull me over. If not, move along." He threatened me physically. I pointed down the road and said, "Let's do it! Meet me in the bank parking lot."

I took side streets toward the bank and found that he wasn't there. Again, another example of road rage and poor judgment. Who knows what would have happened had he shown up? Was he angry and armed? He may have been.

Another incident of road rage occurred in Franklin, Wisconsin. I had two dogs with me in the car when a pickup truck was riding my tail, about a foot from my rear bumper. Being the hothead I was, I gave him a gesture and he moved even closer to my bumper. So I gave him the "let's go" motion. He passed me, got in front of me, and cut me off. I motioned for him to pull over—I was ready to fight—but he chose to move on. I actively looked for his vehicle for at least the next month. In my anger and foolishness, I wanted to get revenge.

While I was working for a health care company in Milwaukee, I was cut off by a vehicle where the road narrowed from two lanes to one. The driver gave no signal or wave and, by nature, that upset me. I often thought people were intentionally messing with me or simply not respecting me, and I invited challenge time and again.

Further ahead, the road widened into two lanes and then merged back into one, where I cut him off. He laid on his horn and gestured. I laughed. However, at the next intersection, he exited his vehicle and approached my door. I lowered my window about five inches, and he raged, "I should pull you out and rough you up!"

"Now sir, there's no reason for that. What's the problem?" I asked innocently.

"You cut me off with no signal!"

"Oh, much like you did to me a mile or so back? Let's move on. Have a good day!"

I closed my window as he was screaming, "I now know where you work!"

I was ready to drive on and noticed he had his teenage son in the car with him. "Great role model!" I yelled.

Choices have consequences.

As you can see, I would often get angry while driving, so much so that I'd punch the steering wheel with my left hand while yelling, "This is not fun! I cannot take this anymore!"

I cared so much what other people might be thinking that I'd try to look calm and cool on the outside while raging on the inside. The lies of the enemy of our souls that lead to paranoia led me to scream in my head, *Stop looking at me and stop mocking me!* My head was full of lies and coercing—but still I had the choice each time to do the right thing or to do the wrong thing.

> **Life Lesson #50:** The high road faces upward, toward the face of God who sees and knows every thought, every detail of our lives, and still loves us with an "everlasting love" (Jeremiah 31:3).

I'm so thankful for truth. The truth about God's love and the truth about our holy, forgiving, merciful, transforming Father, God, and the Savior of our souls, His Son, Jesus. He is transforming my life! I'm continuing to learn how to be better equipped against the devil and his lies and better about loving and forgiving others, for the Word of God tells us, "Love your enemies and pray for those who persecute you" (Matthew 5:44).

> Since God so loved us, we also ought to love one another.
>
> —1 John 4:11

I was a prideful man, which doesn't fly with God, who humbled Himself to become a servant for us, the greatest example of loving others.

> Do nothing from rivalry or conceit, but in humility count others more significant than yourselves. Let each of you look not only to his own interests, but also to the interests of others.
>
> —Philippians 2:3–4

> Hatred stirs up strife, but love covers all offenses.
>
> —Proverbs 10:12

There are countless such scriptures. I would also like to share my personal driving tips, as so many people are angry when driving, like I used to be.

1. Leave early for your destination.
2. Wear a seatbelt at all times.
3. Be patient!
4. Don't text and drive; don't drink and drive.
5. Show grace. You do not know what another driver is going through. Among many possible scenarios, he or she could be dealing with a family emergency, could have just gotten bad news from their doctor, could be having car mechanical issues, or could be dealing with the difficulties of old age. You just never know!

I'm so thankful that I've come to know Jesus and that I'm being transformed day by day. Do you know Him? If not, I urge you to make the following prayer your own to God, receiving His free gift of salvation by simply having faith in Jesus.

> *Dear Lord Jesus, I know I am a sinner. I believe You died for my sins. Right now, I turn from my sins and open the door of my heart and life. I confess You as my personal Lord and Savior. Thank You for saving me. Amen.*[11] – Pastor Greg Laurie

---

11 Pastor Greg Laurie, "How to Know God." *Harvest: https://harvest.org/know-god/how-to-know-god* (November 16, 2019).

16 Lead Me to the Cross

While I was a homeowner in Greendale, I seldom mowed the lawn or shoveled snow because I was afraid my neighbors were watching and criticizing me. In my paranoia, I pictured them standing at their windows, sipping coffee, and saying, "That Paul doesn't seem too swift or handy. Look at him. Not a very good homeowner."

I once had a good two feet of snow in my driveway. My snow-thrower wasn't working, and I wasn't all that handy at fixing things. I was shoveling away and became so angry and paranoid that I threw the shovel in the air, declaring, "I'm done!" I watched TV and ignored the two feet of snow that would prevent me from leaving home. My thought was apathetic and justifying: *Oh well, it'll eventually melt.*

I was particularly obsessed with thoughts of two male neighbors criticizing me for not being a handyman. Those neighbors were often tending to their lawns and making home improvements. I thought they were thinking, *Paul should really sell that home. Home ownership isn't for everybody.*

My serious mental health issues included severe depression that incessantly gripped me. I'd stay up late watching sports. The later I stayed awake the longer I could sleep in, which messed with my body's natural clock. I'd often awake in panic, thinking I couldn't land a good-paying job or career because of my mental illness. *Who would want to hire a man with severe anxiety and fear of committing to an employer?* I would continuously and mercilessly beat myself up.

I dreaded mornings because I'd awake feeling unworthy and had zero desire to shower or work. Sometimes I'd go days without brushing my teeth or taking a shower. I just didn't care. Apathy had set in and I felt hopeless. These signs are among the hallmarks of severe depression. My self-talk was always negative. I kept repeating, *I cannot land a good job!*

Among other poor choices, I was daily watching pornography, which was an addiction until 2008.

> **Life Lesson #51:** Watching pornography means you're giving in to the flesh rather than following the path of righteousness that believers have in Jesus. This life will one day end and we will stand before our Creator. Why spend this life living against His goodness and the blessings that can be reaped from obeying Him?

> We take the good things God has given us and turn them into sin, whether it be involving ourselves in sex that leads to pornography, buying a prostitute for an evening of lust, misusing our money by

> gambling, overconsuming alcohol (which leads to all kinds of trouble, as you've read here in my testimony), or eating unhealthily, which leads to obesity and perpetuates the lie that we have no value and nothing to offer.

Giving in to sexual temptation—immorality by God's protective and loving standards—is the mentally ill, emotionally ill, and spiritually ill way to *feel* valued, accepted, and loved without a root system that sustains life (remember the willow tree). Living by our flesh nature instead of by God's nature is not freeing, not valuing, and not *truly* being loved by others. Sin reaps temporary satisfaction and long-term illness. Sin is simply not worth it! I know this because I've reaped the consequences of my poor decisions made out of ungodly thinking. I knew what was right and wrong, but I found myself still giving in to the flesh.

The guilt I felt after inappropriate sexual relations was tremendous. Why? Guilt is an emotion God created in us—like a flashing red traffic light—to tell us we're doing something wrong, something unhealthy, something outside the boundaries He set for our utmost wellbeing and safety. That feeling of guilt in us is the Holy Spirit convicting us of our sin and warning us that we have moved outside His *protection.*

Sin is sin, and it's defined by our Creator: "If anyone, then, knows the good they ought to do and doesn't do it, it is sin for them" (James 4:17). Who are we to question our Creator? We were all born into sin. "Just as sin entered the world through one man, and death through sin, and in this way death came to all people, because all sinned" (Romans 5:12). We each need the Savior, Jesus.

Instead of spending time watching filth, I could have been reading a book, exercising, and taking part in other wholesome activities that encourage mental, emotional, physical, and spiritual health. Praise God, I learned I could *overcome addictions*! The truth is, you can too! I threw away the pornography videos and began spending my time doing productive and meaningful things. It's a choice!

Let's take a look at what the Bible says about my biggest weakness (temptation)—sexual immorality.

> Do not be deceived: Neither the sexually immoral nor idolaters nor adulterers nor men who have sex with men nor thieves nor the greedy nor drunkards nor slanderers nor swindlers will inherit the kingdom of God. And that is what some of you were. But you were washed, you were sanctified, you were justified in the name of the Lord Jesus Christ and by the Spirit of our God.
>
> "I have the right to do anything," you say—but not everything is beneficial. "I have the right to do anything"—but I will not be mastered by anything. You say, "Food for the stomach and the stomach for food, and God will destroy them both." The body, however, is not meant for sexual immorality but for the Lord, and the Lord for the body. . . .
>
> Flee from sexual immorality. All other sins a person commits are outside the body, but whoever sins sexually, sins against their own body. Do you not know that your bodies are temples of the Holy Spirit, who is in you, whom you have received from God? You are not your own; you were bought at a price. Therefore honor God with your bodies.
>
> —1 Corinthians 6:9–13, 18–20

"From the heart come evil thoughts, murder, adultery, all sexual immorality, theft, lying, and slander."

—Matthew 15:19

"From within, out of a person's heart, come evil thoughts, sexual immorality, theft, murder."

—Mark 7:21

"Abstain from eating food offered to idols, from sexual immorality, from eating the meat of strangled animals, and from consuming blood."

—Acts 15:20

"You must abstain from eating food offered to idols, from consuming blood or the meat of strangled animals, and from sexual immorality. If you do this, you will do well."

—Acts 15:29

I can hardly believe the report about the sexual immorality going on among you—something that even pagans don't do. I am told that a man in your church is living in sin with his stepmother.

—1 Corinthians 5:1

Because there is so much sexual immorality, each man should have his own wife, and each woman should have her own husband.

—1 Corinthians 7:2

We must not engage in sexual immorality as some of them did, causing 23,000 of them to die in one day.

—1 Corinthians 10:8

Yes, I am afraid that when I come again, God will humble me in your presence. And I will be grieved because many of you have not given up your old sins. You have not repented of your impurity, sexual immorality, and eagerness for lustful pleasure.

—2 Corinthians 12:21 (Paul speaking to believers)

When you follow the desires of your sinful nature, the results are very clear: sexual immorality, impurity, lustful pleasures.

—Galatians 5:19

Let there be no sexual immorality, impurity, or greed among you. Such sins have no place among God's people.

—Ephesians 5:3

Put to death the sinful, earthly things lurking within you. Have nothing to do with sexual immorality, impurity, lust, and evil desires. Don't be greedy, for a greedy person is an idolater, worshiping the things of this world.

—Colossians 3:5

Don't forget Sodom and Gomorrah and their neighboring towns, which were filled with immorality and every kind of sexual perversion. Those cities were destroyed by fire and serve as a warning of the eternal fire of God's judgment.

—Jude 1:7

They did not repent of their murders or their witchcraft or their sexual immorality or their thefts.

—Revelation 9:21

All the striving for perfection, the procrastinating, the anger and unforgiveness, the overconsumption of alcohol, the fighting, wooing women, being sexually immoral—I was living life in the moment of sinful pleasure, afraid of death and afraid of living. Through the freedom of salvation and working hard on myself with Jesus by my side and the Holy Spirit's guidance, I can now live less afraid and more at peace knowing that Jesus loves me and has saved me and forgiven my sins. Yes, I still struggle with lust, and I often doubt God's grace, love, and mercy because there are very real trials in life that continue to hit me as they do every individual.

> **Life Lesson #52**: I heard in church, "There's more grace in Christ than sin in me."

> "'For in him we live and move and have our being.' As some of your own poets have said, 'We are his offspring'" (Acts 17:28).

• • •

While in bed one night, feeling miserable and hopeless, I retrieved a cross from a drawer and clenched it in my hand because my sins and mental illness had overcome me. *Lord, lead me to the cross!* At church, I learned of a website that holds people accountable to not viewing pornography: www.xxxchurch.com promotes and offers accountability—holding one another responsible if they waver. We each need accountability partners for any issue of sin we habitually contend with. They also offer small groups and workshops. I came to realize I need others to help me adhere to the importance of leading a moral (godly) life.

> **Life Lesson #53**: Obedience to God is essential to truly living an abundant life as a Christian—a Christ follower. Again, "To obey is better than sacrifice" (1 Samuel 15:22).

His truth sure helps me in daily life! I'm not perfect—none of us are nor will we ever be in this life, but we each can know the truths of God and choose to repent and live under His grace (favor), His forgiveness, and His goodness.

Praise God, I've not viewed pornography since 2008, and I don't miss it! I would rather read, write, watch sports, exercise, coach baseball, be involved in my church, and participate in other healthy activities. The longer I'm sober from pornography, the less I want to watch it. It is finished. Challenge yourself to do the same.

> **Life Lesson #54**: We have to *want* sin to end and *want* to sweep the enemy from our heads in order to conquer the sin in our lives.

> "Submit yourselves, then, to God. Resist the devil, and he will flee from you. Come near to God and he will come near to you. Wash your hands, you sinners, and purify your hearts, you double-minded" (James 4:7–8).

Challenge yourself to abolish pornography and other addictions from your life. Many men (and women) struggle with pornography and an addiction to pornography, but we are each responsible for our choices and addictions. You can overcome addictions and sinful tendencies if you truly want to and you're willing to put in the work. Spend your time in exercise and in reading clean and meaningful material.

There are at least *fifty promises* of God to those who choose to live "right"—not perfectionistic but *right* according to God's Word. Here is just a brief sampling of His promises:

> The eyes of the Lord are on the righteous, and his ears are attentive to their cry.
>
> —Psalm 34:15

> Whoever pursues righteousness and love finds life, prosperity and honor.
>
> —Proverbs 21:21

> For the Lord loves the just and will not forsake his faithful ones. Wrongdoers will be completely destroyed; the offspring of the wicked will perish.
>
> —Psalm 37:28

> Let us not become weary in doing good, for at the proper time we will reap a harvest if we do not give up.
>
> —Galatians 6:9

• • •

I still struggle with lust and the flesh. I find many women beautiful. I am really praying and taking action to further overcome the sin of lust. In that effort, I highly recommend *Every Man's Battle* by Stephen Arterburn and Fred Stoeker. I do occasionally stumble and backslide. The key is to not allow our sins to control us. We must put sin to death by renewing our minds. We become what we think, and we become what we do. We are each responsible for our actions. We can't blame others for our sin choices. Is sexual immorality really worth an unwanted pregnancy, a sexually transmitted disease (STD), or the guilt and remorse that follow a sexual encounter? No.

I had a pregnancy scare just prior to moving to Colorado. It was an awful feeling as I did not love the woman. Although I'm human and tempted by lust, I now act on the fact that there are consequences for my actions.

I want to be obedient to God's Word and avoid sexual immorality, other sin, and their debilitating consequences.

It's up to each of us to decide how we spend our time, what we watch on TV, what we listen to . . . I recommend working, exercising, reading God's Word, watching sports and other clean programming, and listening to Christian music. I used to listen to heavy metal but as I've grown older and wiser I now prefer to listen to classical jazz, sports radio, and Christian music. The point is this: feed your mind good things, not the filth and corruption of this fallen world.

17

Serving Others

I liked to think I had a heart for God. But did I? I had done volunteer work over the years, including as a youth mentor in Milwaukee for ten years and as a statistician for a high school varsity football team. But I was also a sinner in need of a Savior at that time so no, I didn't have a heart for God. No amount of "good deeds" connects our hearts and lives to God. It is only through faith in Jesus and proclaiming Him as Savior that the gap to God is bridged and a heart for God and unity with Him is possible.

> **Life Lesson #55:** "For it is by grace you have been saved, through faith—and this is not from yourselves, it is the gift of God—not by works, so that no one can boast" (Ephesians 2:8–9).

As a mentor, I was matched with a young man for nearly ten years. We had some good times and I like to believe I was a good influence. But severe anxiety and doubt created a continuum of paranoid questions. *What if his mother thinks I'm a pedophile? What if we get into an accident? What if he gets bored with me?*

As a statistician for my friend's high school football team, I experienced perhaps some of the worst social anxiety of my life: I believed I had to look tough and cool in front of the football team, coaches, fans, and staff. When talking with the staff, I wondered what negative thoughts about me were playing out in their minds and being whispered about me in the stands.

Why did I subject myself to such mental anguish? I hadn't played high school football, so I believed the players and coaches thought I was emotionally weak and didn't know the game well. That lie made me want to get into confrontations and fights. I tried to appear calm and cool, but there was always a fire burning inside me. *What if someone asks about the previous play and I didn't see what had happened? What if my statistics aren't perfect? What if I'm not asked to come back the next season to help out?* It was mentally exhausting.

After Friday night games, the coaching staff, spouses, and significant others would go out for food and drinks. I had such extreme social anxiety when joining them that I would worry, *Who should I talk to? What should I say? Who's judging me? Should I just leave? What am I doing here? What are they saying about me?* Thank the Lord, just prior to leaving for Colorado in late 2011, I attended a high school football playoff game and was unprecedentedly calm on the sidelines because I had prayed for peace of mind and repeatedly reminded myself the truth: *I belong to Jesus. He bought me with the price of His own life so I would no longer be condemned in my sin of human nature.* That peace was freeing. We went out afterward for food and drinks and I had minimal social anxiety. I knew then that through Jesus and His empowering Spirit in me, I could and would overcome!

I've tasted victory and I believe you can too. Victory over our hurts and sins begins with a dedicated relationship with Jesus and a loyal love for God that persuades us to follow His Word. In return, we reap the joys of His promises.

For a number of years, I was a volunteer for another organization as well. I met some good people, but again, that provoked a lot of social anxiety. I threw myself into these social situations in hope of overcoming. Why else would I subject myself to such emotional anxiety and mental torture? I wonder what would have become of me had I not forced myself to get out and socialize while trusting in my heavenly Father to help me overcome. I don't want to know what evil I could have caused.

News reports no longer shock me. Our world needs the transforming power of Jesus to defeat the enemy of our souls, but each individual on Planet Earth must make that personal decision to accept Jesus as Savior and then to be proactive in following and obeying His Word.

As I've grown older, more mature, wiser, and more familiar with the Bible, I've come to realize the importance of faith, forgiveness, and repentance. It's important to learn from our past as long as we don't continue to live in it. I lived in my past for far too long. I spent many days in bed, eating unhealthy foods, being alone and depressed, letting life pass me by while I watched sports on TV. Watching sports is great, but it has its place in the balance of a fuller life, which should include healthy habits across the board and Jesus at the center.

God is molding me into the man He wants me to be for His glory and purposes. I can now thank Him for everything

I've experienced because I've learned from those experiences. The past is a great learning tool to help us live better today and tomorrow. We may have some regrets, but what good does it do to beat ourselves up over things past? We must learn from our past mistakes but live in the present and move forward as active Christ followers.

> Forget the former things; do not dwell on the past.
>
> –Isaiah 43:18

I used to think my life was a waste of time, but not anymore. I've been reborn by Jesus and I'm choosing daily to live as a Christian—a Christ follower. The term "Christian" has become gravely diluted, so it's important to remember that simply calling yourself a Christian versus actually walking out your days as a true Christ follower are two very different things.

> **Life Lesson #56:** Live in the moment with Jesus and make the most of each day because we are not guaranteed tomorrow.

In August 2010, I went on a church mission trip to the Dominican Republic, an excellent and eye-opening life experience. A group of us from church helped build a church in Santiago. We stayed in a dorm with no amenities. I was thankful just to have a bed!

At the construction site we moved dirt, poured concrete, pulled weeds, loaded trucks with stone—a great workout. The mission trip gave me a new perspective on life. I realized how fortunate we are as Americans to have the basics: potable water, toilets that can handle the flushing of toilet paper, contemporary sewer systems, and nice baseball fields!

The poverty, filth, and garbage in the Dominican Republic

are overwhelming and depressing, but somehow the poor manage to smile and love. With so few material things, it's amazing how they seem so happy. Maybe just having a relationship with Jesus is enough for them. It's enough for each of us but we forget this truth: Like the disadvantaged in third-world countries, you and I don't need the newest smartphone, car, outfit, or home. Those are temporary things.

> **Life Lesson #57**: "For our light and momentary troubles are achieving for us an eternal glory that far outweighs them all. So we fix our eyes not on what is seen, but on what is unseen, since what is seen is temporary, but what is unseen is eternal" (2 Corinthians 4:17–18). Americans are truly blessed.

We spent a couple of days in what is referred to as "The Hole"—a neighborhood full of starving children and families, drug abuse, prostitution, garbage, pigs on the loose, and emaciated dogs. The dogs made me think of how Bruno at that time had a better life than the people. Yet the children we met at the feeding center were bursting with life, love, and laughter. Some would run up to us, but I felt I didn't deserve that unconditional love and acceptance. Amazingly, though they were very poor and knew only a physical life of filth and poverty, they still had generous smiles and hugs to give. The experience made me feel both sad and thankful—thankful for their testimonies, thankful for the experience of seeing my own life through a different lens, and thankful for all I have and my ability to give to those in need. The Dominican Republic children of The Hole demonstrated this scripture to me:

> Give thanks in all circumstances; for this is God's will for you in Christ Jesus.
>
> —1 Thessalonians 5:18

• • •

Late In 2010, I felt absolutely at a dead end. While meeting yet again with a psychiatrist, I realized that enough was enough and I needed to do something drastic. I had often thought of exercising, but thinking isn't doing. That day I went right from my psychiatrist's office to an athletic club and joined—and I became a regular in spin class. I felt so much better about myself after a good workout. I thanked God and also began tithing to my church.

I don't recall ever feeling better in my life than when I was exercising consistently and tithing—giving back a portion of what God has graciously given me to further the purposes of His church. Exercising and giving . . . I was onto something!

Conversely, I thought if I missed a tithe, it was too late to get back on track. Or if I missed a workout, it was too late to resume.

> **Life Lesson #58:** Live one day at a time. Exercise and tithe to your local church. Get a daily planner and plan your week of work, exercise, and tithing. You won't miss that financial gift to God. Besides, it isn't your money in the first place—it belongs to Him. Tithing is an act of worship and gratitude to God that He will multiply. His red-letter promise is "Give, and it will be given to you. A good measure, pressed down, shaken together and running over, will be poured into your lap. For with the measure you use, it will be measured to you" (Luke 6:38).

I began most days by reading Scripture and a devotion. I'd found how important it is to feed often from the living bread of the Bible.

> Taste and see that the Lord is good; blessed is the one who takes refuge in him.
>
> —Psalm 34:8

I experience great peace of mind reading God's Word. It reminds me to focus on Jesus rather than myself and to forgive others who have wronged and hurt me. After all, God forgave me—all my past, present, and future sins were nailed to the cross—so who am I to not forgive others? I'm grateful that through faith in Jesus He has forgiven me and removed my sins "as far as the east is from the west" (Psalm 103:12) and no longer remembers them (Hebrews 8:12). I'm grateful He extends incomprehensible love, care, and patience to me (He has certainly been longsuffering). So who am I to not extend love, care, and patience to others? This is how amazing our Creator is!

Reading God's Word motivates me to lead others to Jesus and help those who are in practical need. Look at the daily news. So much hurt and sin are in this fallen world, but there is *living and lasting hope* in Jesus! Don't believe the lies that you have nothing to offer others. Believers in Jesus have everything awesome to offer!

> **Life Lesson #59**: God has gifted each of us. He is ever present and in control. Every good gift comes from Him (James 1:17) and with Him "all things are possible" (Matthew 19:26).

18

FINAL THOUGHTS

I'd like to share some final tips and advice with you. I was living life afraid of death, and that's not true living. Men and women struggling with serious mental health issues, I urge you to get a Bible, get a job, find a local church home, get counseling, and get a gym membership—in that order—and get a group of friends for socialization who are mature Christ followers. True believers will pray for you and with you, cheer you forward, and hold you accountable.

I urge everyone to . . .

- Commit your life to Jesus and walk out His Word.
- Find a solid Bible-believing church and tithe to God through that church.
- Commit to reading the Bible and a daily devotion.
- "Rejoice always, *pray without ceasing,* in everything give thanks; for this is the will of God in Christ Jesus for you" (1 Thessalonians 5:16–18).

- Find a good Christian counselor and take only necessary and beneficial medications—bearing in mind that you will not find life's answers in medication, as I've shown through my life story.
- Stay out of debt.
- Obtain good health insurance.
- Ask for help when you need it.
- Listen to positive songs and Christian music.
- Eat a healthy diet.
- Exercise.
- Make wise decisions.
- Limit alcohol and caffeine intake.
- Be thankful for all you have.
- Forgive yourself and others.
- Love yourself and others as God does!

I could not keep living in fear of death; I'd had enough of that. Jesus overcame sin and death, the war of evil has already been won, and we will see that victory in our world when Jesus returns. Believers in Jesus, we are simply passing through this life on our way to eternal life with the Lord. Don't live this life afraid of death—our physical death leads to eternal life with God! My struggles with mental health have been difficult, but I am victorious through Jesus!

Prayer and positive affirmations will help you renew your mind. The transformation of how we think, which leads to decisions and actions, will not happen overnight. However, it's been proven time and again that we can retrain our brains—and with the indwelling power of the Holy Spirit of God, we cannot be stopped!

> Being confident of this, that he who began a good work in you will carry it on to completion until the day of Christ Jesus.
>
> —Philippians 1:6

Be consistent, be persistent, and never give up. God has an incredible plan for your life; you just need to submit to Him, to His Word, to His goodness, and to His never-ending perfect love.

Here are my positive affirmations that may help you in your journey to become Christlike. Some are particular to my paranoid tendency. I urge you to list and repeat your own positive affirmations that align with God's Word, especially when going into challenging circumstances.

- I have faith in Jesus as my Lord and Savior. (1 John 5:5)
- I am forgiven for all my sins through Jesus. (Acts 13:38–39)
- I repent of my many sins. (1 John 1:9)
- I must be obedient to God's Word. (James 1:22)
- God will provide me with employment and a career. (Philippians 4:19)
- God wants me to show His kindness and love to others. (1 Peter 4:8)
- I will not feel guilty. I will give my regrets to Jesus. (Romans 8:1)
- I will put God first always. (Matthew 6:33)
- I have the mind of Jesus. (1 Corinthians 2:16)
- I am set apart by Jesus. (Hebrews 10:10–12)

- I am worthy, and if it is God's will, He will send me a godly woman I deserve to marry. (Matthew 7:9–11)
- I am not responsible for others' thoughts, behaviors, or words, (Galatians 6:5)
- I do not know what others are thinking; they have better things to do than to focus on me. (Romans 12:16)
- Others are not staring at me when I eat; I will not choke. (Joshua 1:9; Philippians 4:6–7; 2 Timothy 1:7)
- If others think of me in negative terms, that's okay. I know who I am in Jesus. (2 Corinthians 5:17)
- If others criticize me, that's okay. Jesus was criticized. There is no need for me to be critical of myself or others. The persecuted are blessed by God. (Matthew 5:10)
- Others are not mocking, judging, or ridiculing me; they are focused on their own lives. (Hebrews 13:6)
- If others ridicule me, that's okay. Jesus was ridiculed. The persecuted are blessed by God. (Matthew 5:10)
- I have the gift of knowledge. (Proverbs 2:6)
- I may not be right, but that's okay. (1 John 1:9)
- I am kind and intelligent. (Matthew 7:18)
- I enjoy social situations because God created me for fellowship. (1 John 1:7)
- What I say is worthy and valid; I enjoy talking and sharing my opinion in social settings. (Luke 6:38)

- There is no need for me to feel defensive at all times. (Colossians 3:1–2)
- I can focus on the task at hand. (Proverbs 16:3)
- I am not afraid to ask others for help. (Romans 12:5)
- I do not need to rethink or rewrite everything. (Isaiah 26:3)
- I like to laugh even when others do not think it's funny. (Proverbs 17:22)
- I am fit and losing weight. (Philippians 4:13)
- I will not interrupt others. (James 1:19)
- I will make mistakes, but that's okay. That's how we learn. (Proverbs 24:16)
- I am not nosy, rude, or inappropriate. I am respectful and compassionate. (Colossians 3:12)

A Message to Children

Stand up for yourself and open up. Do not give in to peer pressure to do immoral or illegal things. I encourage you to play multiple sports or join band or whatever healthy activity you enjoy. Making a mistake in life does not mean you're stupid. Do your best at whatever you do but realize that mistakes are made by everyone every day, and those mistakes are opportunities to learn.

A Message to Adults

Deal with your anger in healthy, productive ways; challenge yourself not to watch pornography and to rid your surroundings of pornography. Get involved in youth activities such as coaching sports or helping in youth groups and clubs.

A Message to Fathers and Husbands

Your role is vital in the lives of your children, so spend quality time with them. Love and respect your wives. Be leaders at home. Be at home with your family at night and not out drinking with your friends. It's okay occasionally to have a beer with the boys, but your family needs you first and foremost and is depending on you. Man up. Go home.

A Message to Those Battling Any Form of Mental Health Issues

Know that God loves you! I love you too, and we can get through this together. I believe the root of our mental illness is sin. We are all sinners in need of a Savior.

I couldn't have written my story without first gaining a personal relationship with Jesus, and I couldn't save my soul. But Jesus did because I called out to God in faith for salvation, believing in His Son, Jesus. "Believe in the Lord Jesus, and you will be saved" (Acts 16:31).

A Message to All Readers

Laugh! Proverbs 17:22 says, "A cheerful heart is good medicine," and Ecclesiastes 3:4 says there is "a time to laugh." Focus on the things that bring you joy and enjoy the things that make you laugh. What makes me laugh are *Seinfeld*, *The King of Queens*, and comedians Jim Gaffigan and Brian Regan. For youth, I recommend Looney Tunes for laughs! Yes, I still watch cartoons in my forties. I enjoy Boomerang and Cartoon Network. Never too old!

I pray that my transparency through this book will lead you and countless others to Jesus and the abundant life and eternal life He offers to all who will believe in Him.

19

"Good Night. Love You. See You in the Morning."

I have lived in many places in my adulthood, often looking for a better place to live, a better job, a better life. As for living arrangements, I didn't want to be alone because I feared this would bring even more isolation and depression. These are awful feelings. I needed the love and support of others in my daily life. My nieces, Kiley and Lindsay, for example, mean the world to me, and every once in a while, despite my serious mental health issues, I'd think, *They are the reason not to take my life.* I love them so much. I love those times when, just before they'd go to bed, they'd say to me, "Good night. Love you. See you in the morning." They are one of the many reasons I wrote this book—out of love.

I also wrote my life story for personal reasons. The writing served as a time of self-reflection and a freeing, therapeutic walk with Jesus. And I really enjoy writing. But mainly I wrote this book for the young boys and girls out there who are struggling right now, to encourage them to realize it's good to share your feelings, it's okay to make mistakes, to not be perfect, and to seek help. Life is tough and it can be extraordinarily tough at a young age.

Along my perfectly imperfect walk, I discovered that Satan doesn't have the power to make me do anything. I get to choose. So as it turned out, I was the problem all along by not choosing God and not being obedient to Him. What caused my forty-year battle with severe anxiety and chronic depression? I believe these are the causes:

- my sinful nature (especially drunkenness and sexual immorality)
- my eye injury
- a dysfunctional childhood
- a lack of obedience and self-control
- a lack of intense exercise

Again, let's look at both parts of John 10:10, as we each get to choose one of two paths in life:

1. A life of poor thinking that leads to poor choices, sin, guilt, regrets, destruction, anxiety, anger, and depression—the path of your enemy, Satan, that leads to a dead-end and death. "The thief comes only to steal and kill and destroy" (John 10:10, part 1).
2. A life in Jesus that produces the fruit of the Spirit: "love, joy, peace, forbearance, kindness, goodness, faithfulness, gentleness and self-control" (Galatians 5:22–23). "I have come that they may have life, and have it to the full" (John 10:10 part 2).

I highly recommend the second path. I challenge you to choose God's team. And I highly recommend these practical self-care steps and coping skills:

Self-care:

- Get outdoors.
- Take a walk.
- Stretch.
- Get a massage.
- Consider acupuncture.
- Watch a movie.
- Listen to jazz music.
- Attend church.
- Be grateful.
- Laugh.

Coping skills:

- Do breathing exercises.
- Manage your time.
- Take a walk.
- Exercise.
- Get enough sleep.
- Eat healthy.
- Read.
- Socialize.
- Dog-sit.
- Talk to someone.

Try as we may, none of us is perfect, but we now know where to turn when our walk becomes unbearable: Jesus and His followers. Through thick and thin and all my sin, Jesus has been there all along with me. It's true what He said: "Never will I leave you; never will I forsake you" (Hebrews 13:5).

Looking back, I see that my life has been *A Perfect Walk* all along. As imperfect as it was to me, it was a perfect walk with the Lord, the perfect walk that led me to transformation and eternal life. May God bless us all in our walk with Him.

> *Thank You, God. Without Your allowing me to go through adversity, I would not have turned my life over to You. I would not have this opportunity to help others find You. And I would not have the opportunity to help those who are suffering from debilitating anxiety disorders to find the only true path to healing: Your Son, Jesus.*

To sum up this book, I have concluded the following about myself and mankind as a whole:

> **Life Lesson #60:** The problem is me, but the solution is Jesus. God the Father allows things to happen in our lives to bring glory to Him.

You may have read this book because you're one of my relatives, friends, or former coworkers. My hope is that whoever you are and whatever you're doing in this short life, this book will help you realize the importance of truth—God's truth—in making good decisions. You will never regret surrendering your life to Jesus, and I pray you will choose Him as the center of your life if you haven't already. He is the best decision I've ever made.

Love the Lord more than you enjoy your sin.

Following Jesus can be frustrating and overwhelming, but the reward is eternal. I have days when I wonder if God is truly for me. At times I still ask, *Does God really care? Why does He not answer my prayers? Does He know I'm suffering greatly? When will this end? When will He rid my mind completely of all the lies I've bought into for almost forty years?* This is where faith and believing enter. Like the apostle Paul, I've concluded that I suffer greatly for Jesus, and it's an honor to do so. I also often suffer because of a lack of obedience to God as my Father. Paul wrote, "Here is a trustworthy saying that deserves full acceptance: Jesus came into the world to save sinners—of whom I am the worst" (1 Timothy 1:15).

I love the truths of "Who I Am in Christ," compiled by author Neil Anderson:

> I AM ACCEPTED...
>
> John 1:12 I am God's child.
>
> John 15:15 As a disciple, I am a friend of Jesus Christ.
>
> Romans 5:1 I have been justified (declared righteous).
>
> 1 Corinthians 6:17 I am united with the Lord, and I am one with Him in spirit.
>
> 1 Corinthians 6:19-20 I have been bought with a price and I belong to God.
>
> 1 Corinthians 12:27 I am a member of Christ's body.
>
> Ephesians 1:3-8 I have been chosen by God and adopted as His child.
>
> Colossians 1:13-14 I have been redeemed and forgiven of all my sins.

Colossians 2:9-10 I am complete in Christ.

Hebrews 4:14-16 I have direct access to the throne of grace through Jesus Christ.

I AM SECURE . . .

Romans 8:1-2 I am free from condemnation.

Romans 8:28 I am assured that God works for my good in all circumstances.

Romans 8:31-39 I am free from any condemnation brought against me and I cannot be separated from the love of God.

2 Corinthians 1:21-22 I have been established, anointed and sealed by God.

Colossians 3:1-4 I am hidden with Christ in God.

Philippians 1:6 I am confident that God will complete the good work He started in me.

Philippians 3:20 I am a citizen of heaven.

2 Timothy 1:7 I have not been given a spirit of fear but of power, love and a sound mind.

1 John 5:18 I am born of God and the evil one cannot touch me.

I AM SIGNIFICANT . . .

John 15:5 I am a branch of Jesus Christ, the true vine, and a channel of His life.

John 15:16 I have been chosen and appointed to bear fruit.

1 Corinthians 3:16 I am God's temple.

2 Corinthians 5:17-21 I am a minister of reconciliation for God.

Ephesians 2:6 I am seated with Jesus Christ in the heavenly realm.

Ephesians 2:10 I am God's workmanship.

Ephesians 3:12 I may approach God with freedom and confidence.

Philippians 4:13 I can do all things through Christ, who strengthens me.[12]

• • •

A good friend suggested I end this book with Scripture. Please keep in mind that this friend means a lot to me and I often pray he will start going to church. He, like me and all of us, is a sinner in need of healing. I once wrote his name on a stone at a church in Milwaukee when we were asked to write the name of an individual we were praying would one day turn to Jesus. I believe my friend will one day walk through the front doors of a church and begin his walk with the Lord. And I am quite sure I will cry tears of joy and gratitude to God in that moment.

I urge you to memorize the following scriptures. These two passages have been most significant in ministering to my worrisome nature and complex thought processes.

> Do not be anxious about anything, but in every situation, by prayer and petition, with thanksgiving,

---

12 Neal Anderson, "Who I Am in Christ." *VintageLawrence.com: https://vintagelawrence.com/wp-content/uploads/2013/01/ANDERSON_WhoIAmInChrist.pdf* (January 16, 2020).

> present your requests to God. And the peace of God, which transcends all understanding, will guard your hearts and your minds in Christ Jesus.
>
> —Philippians 4:6–7

> Do not conform to the pattern of this world, but be transformed by the renewing of your mind. Then you will be able to test and approve what God's will is—his good, pleasing and perfect will.
>
> —Romans 12:2

There is no better way to end this book than with the encouragement of Jesus through the apostle Paul. Read it and believe.

> I consider that our present sufferings are not worth comparing with the glory that will be revealed in us. For the creation waits in eager expectation for the children of God to be revealed. For the creation was subjected to frustration, not by its own choice, but by the will of the one who subjected it, in hope that the creation itself will be liberated from its bondage to decay and brought into the freedom and glory of the children of God.

> We know that the whole creation has been groaning as in the pains of childbirth right up to the present time. Not only so, but we ourselves, who have the firstfruits of the Spirit, groan inwardly as we wait eagerly for our adoption to sonship, the redemption of our bodies. For in this hope we were saved. But hope that is seen is no hope at all. Who hopes for what they already have? But if we hope for what we do not yet have, we wait for it patiently.

In the same way, the Spirit helps us in our weakness. We do not know what we ought to pray for, but the Spirit himself intercedes for us through wordless groans. And he who searches our hearts knows the mind of the Spirit, because the Spirit intercedes for God's people in accordance with the will of God.

And we know that in all things God works for the good of those who love him, who have been called according to his purpose. For those God foreknew he also predestined to be conformed to the image of his Son, that he might be the firstborn among many brothers and sisters. And those he predestined, he also called; those he called, he also justified; those he justified, he also glorified.

What, then, shall we say in response to these things? If God is for us, who can be against us?

—Romans 8:18–31

Personal Prayer

Heavenly Father, I have sinned against You countless times. I repent and thank You for Your forgiveness that was granted to me on the cross and to all who believe in Your Son, Jesus. I pray for peace of mind and a heart that overflows with Your love for me. Help me extend Your love and grace to others. Thank You for Your Holy Spirit, who lives in me and in all who believe as counselor, convictor, confidant, comforter, and empowering cornerstone. Father, take this anxiety, anger, and depression—the enemy's tools—from me as I continue to surrender all to Your perfect will, day in and day out. In the name of Jesus I pray. Amen.

Final Exhortation

> Rejoice in the Lord always. I will say it again: Rejoice! Let your gentleness be evident to all. The Lord is near.
>
> —Philippians 4:4–5

Resources to Aid Your Perfectly Imperfect Walk

Bible References for the words *perfect* and *walk*.

"Perfect"	"Walk"
Deuteronomy 32:4	Ephesians 5
Job 36:4	Genesis 17:1
Psalm 19:7	Deuteronomy 5:33
Isaiah 26:3	Joshua 22:5
Matthew 19:21	2 Chronicles 6:31
2 Corinthians 12:9	Psalm 1:1
Colossians 3:14	Proverbs 2:20
Hebrews 5:9	Isaiah 35:8
James 1:17	Hosea 14:9
1 John 4:18	John 8:12

Hotlines and Lifelines

- Anxiety and Depression Association of America, ADAA www.adaa.org
- Substance Abuse and Mental Health Services National Helpline: 800-662-HELP (4357) www.samhsa.gov/find-help/national-helpline
- National Suicide Prevention Hotline www.suicidepreventionlifeline.org

Prayer Request Sites

- VCY America, Prayer Line
  www.vcyamerica.org/prayer-line
- K-Love, Prayer
  www.klove.com/ministry/prayer
- Air1, Prayer Request
  www.air1.com/ministry/prayer-request

National Christ-Centered Support Groups

- Celebrate Recovery Groups Directory
  locator.crgroups.info
- National Association for Christian Recovery
  www.nacr.org/referral-center/finding-a-group
- Christians in Recovery, National Directory
  www.christians-in-recovery.org/Tools_
  Organizations_Groups#Christian

Grow in Your Walk with Jesus—Discipleship

- Bible Questions Answered
  www.gotquestions.org
- Pastor Greg Laurie
  www.harvest.org
- Dr. David Jeremiah
  www.davidjeremiah.org

Manhood/Womanhood

- *A Guide to Biblical Manhood*
  by Randy Stinson
- Authentic Manhood
  www.authenticmanhood.com

- The Council on Biblical Manhood and Womanhood
  www.cbmw.org

Financial Freedom

- Dave Ramsey and Financial Peace University
  www.daveramsey.com/store/financial-peace-university

Healthy Eating

- Eat This, Not That
  www.eatthis.com
- Dr. Bob Marshall, PhD, Radiant Life Nutrition
  www.radiantlightnutrition.com
- Kimberly Taylor, Take Back Your Temple
  www.takebackyourtemple.com

Resources for Youth and High School Baseball Coaches

- Coach and Play Baseball
  www.coachandplaybaseball.com
- Baseball. The Ripken Way.
  www.ripkenbaseball.com
- Pro Baseball Insider
  www.probaseballinsider.com

Author Contact

Email: paul@aperfectwalk.com
Website: www.aperfectwalk.com
Facebook: www.facebook.com/paul.m.gallagher.7
LinkedIn: www.linkedin.com/in/paul-m-gallagher-245b1a120/

Made in the USA
Las Vegas, NV
07 September 2021

29790835R00125